This may also be used with the trainer's
guide and video with the same title.

BUILDING STRUCTURES WITH YOUNG CHILDREN

OTHER BOOKS IN THE YOUNG SCIENTIST SERIES:

building
structures
with
young
children

The
Young
Scientist
Series

Ingrid Chalufour and Karen Worth
Education Development Center, Inc.

Redleaf Press
St. Paul, Minnesota
www.redleafpress.org

Published by Redleaf Press
a division of Resources for Child Caring
10 Yorkton Court
St. Paul, MN 55117
Visit us online at www.redleafpress.org.

Written by Ingrid Chalufour and Karen Worth with Robin Moriarty, Jeffrey Winokur, and Sharon Grollman.

© 2004 Education Development Center, Inc.
Cover and interior design by Percolator.
Interior typeset in Weiss.

Redleaf Press books are available at a special discount when purchased in bulk for special premiums and sales promotions. For details, contact the sales manager at 800-423-8309.

This book was written with the support of National Science Foundation Grant ESI-9818737. However, any opinions, findings, conclusions, and/or recommendations herein are those of the authors and do not necessarily reflect the views of NSF.

Library of Congress Cataloging-in-Publication Data
Chalufour, Ingrid.
  Building structures with young children / Ingrid Chalufour and Karen Worth (Education Development Center, Inc.).—1st ed.
       p. cm.—(The young scientist series)
  Includes bibliographical references and index.
  ISBN 1-929610-50-5 (pbk.)
  1. Building—Study and teaching (Early childhood)—Activity programs. 2. Structural engineering—Study and teaching (Early childhood)—Activity programs. 3. Block building (Children's activity) I. Worth, Karen. II. Education Development Center. III. Title. IV. Series: Chalufour, Ingrid. Young scientist series.

  TH165.C48 2004
  649'.51—dc22

                                                                                          2004005950

Manufactured in the United States of America

11 10 09 08 07 06 05 04   1 2 3 4 5 6 7 8

The Young Scientist Series was developed by a team of early childhood educators at Education Development Center, Inc., which was funded by a grant from the National Science Foundation and led by Ingrid Chalufour and Karen Worth. Listed below are the members of the team, all of whom contributed substantially to the work from its conceptualization to the final product.

INGRID CHALUFOUR has designed and conducted professional development programs for staff in child care programs, Head Start, public schools, and social service agencies for more than thirty-five years.

SHARON GROLLMAN, a senior research associate at EDC's Center for Children and Families, has developed educational materials for more than twenty years. Prior to coming to EDC, she was part of a research team in early childhood education.

ROBIN MORIARTY taught young children in the Boston area for fourteen years before she joined EDC. Currently, her work includes curriculum development, leading professional development programs, and working with early childhood centers.

JEFFREY WINOKUR has worked in early childhood and science education for over twenty years as an instructor in education at Wheelock College and a senior research associate at EDC. He also conducts workshops and training for communities in science for young children.

KAREN WORTH has been a senior scientist at EDC for the past thirty-five years. She is also a graduate-level instructor at Wheelock College in the early childhood education department. Her work includes the development of science curriculum and professional development programs, as well as consultation in science education for young children.

contents

acknowledgments

The Young Scientist Series was developed by the project staff of the Tool Kit for Early Childhood Science Education housed at Education Development Center, Inc. (EDC), with funding from the National Science Foundation.

Numerous educators and consultants contributed to the development and field-testing of the series. We would like to thank the following people for their contributions to this work.

DEVELOPMENT TEACHERS

Cindy Hoisington
Lucia McAlpin
Carole Moyer
Rebecca Palacios
Susan Steinsick

PILOT TEACHERS

Colette Auguste
Liana Bond
Imelda DeCosta
Marlene Dure
Frank Greene
Karen Hoppe
Terry Kuchenmeister
Stuart Lui
Maureen McIntee
Susan Miller
Katherine O'Leary
Carolyn Robinson
Ellen Sulek
Laurie Wormstead
Tiffany Young

FIELD TEST SITES

Bainbridge Island Child Care
    Centers, Bainbridge Island, WA
Barre Town School, Barre, VT
Berlin Elementary School,
    Berlin, VT
Blackwater Community School,
    Coolidge, AZ
Blue Hill Avenue Early Education
    Center, Boston, MA

Bright Horizons at Preston
    Corners, Cary, NC
Childspace Day Care Centers,
    Philadelphia, PA
City of Phoenix Head Start,
    Phoenix, AZ
Cisco Family Connection Bright
    Horizons, Milpitas, CA
East Montpelier Elementary
    School, East Montpelier, VT
Epic Head Start, Yakima, WA
Fort Worth Museum of Science
    and History, Fort Worth, TX
Four Corners School, East
    Montpelier, VT
K–5 Inquiry-Based Science
    Program, Seattle Public
    Schools, WA
Louisiana Tech University Early
    Childhood Education Center,
    Ruston, LA
Motorola Childcare and Education
    Center, Schaumburg, IL
Pasadena Unified School District,
    Pasadena, CA
Phoenix Head Start, Phoenix, AZ
Portage Private Industry Council
    Head Start, Ravenna, OH
School for Early Learning, Spring
    Branch Independent School
    District, Houston, TX
Thomson Early Childhood Center,
    Seattle, WA
UMC Child Development Lab,
    Columbia, MO

Valle Imperial Project in Science,
    El Centro, CA
William H. Rowe School,
    Yarmouth, ME
Young Achievers Science and
    Mathematics Pilot School,
    Boston, MA

ADVISORY BOARD MEMBERS

Douglas Clements
David Dickinson
George Forman
Linda French
Marilou Hyson
Stephanie Johnson
Diane Levin
Mary Jane Moran
Carolyn Vieria
Sandra Williams
Diane Willow

CONSULTANTS

Mary Eisenberg
Pat Fitzsimmons
Ben Mardell
Janet Sebell

We also would like to acknowledge
the following people at EDC:

Erica Fields, Research Assistant
Kerry Ouellet, Editor and
    Production Manager
Susan Weinberg, Senior
    Administrative Assistant

introduction

"In a world filled with the products of scientific inquiry, scientific literacy has become a necessity for everyone. Everyone needs to use scientific information to make choices that arise every day. Everyone needs to be able to engage intelligently in public discourse and debate about important issues that involve science and technology. And everyone deserves to share in the excitement and personal fulfillment that can come from understanding and learning about the natural world" (National Research Council 1996, 1).

"If a child is to keep alive his inborn sense of wonder, he needs the companionship of at least one adult who can share it, rediscovering with him the joy, the excitement, and the mystery of the world" (Carson 1965).

How do we keep alive this inborn sense of wonder in early childhood classrooms? How can teachers provide children with appropriate experiences and guidance? Using the Young Scientist series is one way. But before we describe the series and how to use this guide, we would like to share a few responses to two important questions: (1) Why is science knowledge important? and (2) Why should we start in the preschool years?

Why Is Science Knowledge Important?

One goal of science is to understand the natural world. Knowing some science can help us explain things that happen, such as why water evaporates and why plants grow in particular locations, what causes disease, and how electricity works. Scientific knowledge also can help us predict what might happen—where a hurricane may hit the coast or how severe the flu may be this winter.

But science is more than knowledge; it is also a process of exploration that we call *scientific inquiry*. When scientists try to learn something about events, objects, or materials, they observe, wonder, and ask questions. And they go further and focus on one question, predicting what they think they might find out and setting up an investigation. They observe closely, using their senses and tools to collect and record data and evidence. Through analysis of their data and reflection on all they've done, they develop new ideas and theories and communicate those to others.

Most of us are not scientists, but in many small ways, we do science. When you ask the question, "How much light does my geranium need to flower well?" and then test the different possibilities by putting one in the sun and one in the shade to find the answer, you are doing science. When you compare two pens, predict which one you think will work best for the drawing you are making, and then try them out, you are doing science. When you use a book to find out what kind of birdseed will attract cardinals, you are doing science.

Whether we work in a lab or a school, chart the course of hurricanes, or want to learn about sound, we all have questions—scientists and nonscientists, adults and children alike—and we all use some of the basic tools of scientific inquiry. Given the opportunity to explore and discover, we all can feel the sense of wonder, joy, and excitement that Rachel Carson describes above.

Why Should We Start Science in the Preschool Years?

Children's curiosity about the natural world, their "inborn sense of wonder," is a powerful catalyst for their work and play. With this curiosity and the need to make sense of the world, children are motivated to ask questions, explore how things work, and look closely at the natural world around them.

But in today's world, children's experiences and their opportunities to do science are often limited—confined too frequently to the passive and secondhand experience of the television or video game. Modern technology also has hidden from view some of the basic ways in which things work. Our food comes from stores and few children have seen or engaged in growing and processing it. Toys that were once pushed or pulled or rolled now have hidden motors and batteries to drive them and a switch to turn them on and off.

Science curriculum is important in the early childhood classroom so that "doing science" becomes a natural and critical part of children's early learning. With carefully selected materials and thoughtful guidance, children's explorations will encourage them to observe more closely, develop new ideas about the world, and build a foundation of experiences and ideas on which to construct later understanding. Science in early childhood classrooms also provides a rich context in which children can develop other important skills, including large- and small-muscle control, language and early mathematical understanding, and cooperation.

What Is the Young Scientist Series?

The Young Scientist series is a science curriculum for children who are three to five years old. Each of the teacher guides provides background information and detailed guidance on how to incorporate science into your daily program using many of the materials you already have in the classroom in new ways. *Discovering Nature with Young Children* is about the living things right outside the classroom door. *Exploring Water with Young Children* takes a new look at the water table and *Building Structures with Young Children* challenges children to use building materials found in the classroom to explore questions of how to make things strong,

tall, or elegant. Each study can take several months or extend over longer periods of time.

The Young Scientist series is not about learning and repeating facts, information, and vocabulary with little direct experience. It is not following a set of directed activities or learning the scientific method. It is not a week focused on bears and it is not observing random objects on a science table. The Young Scientist series makes science the work and play of exploring materials and phenomena, while providing opportunities for children to learn from that experience. Young children may do this as they engage in fantasy and dramatic play—creating magic potions at the water table or building a home for the make-believe turtle in the block area. They may do science as they challenge themselves or invent a game: "Who can build the highest tower or empty the water bucket the fastest?" They also may engage in exploration as young scientists, wondering and questioning and seeking to make sense of the world: "What would happen if I rolled the ball from the very top of the ramp? What does my worm need to live? I wonder if I can find an anthill near the one we found yesterday?"

As they explore and interact with one another, young children try to make sense of what they see and do. They develop early theories about why things are the way they are, act the way they do, and how they relate to one another. As their experience broadens and their thinking deepens, their ideas and theories become more plausible and closer to current understandings in science.

Exciting science experiences for young children do not just happen. The Young Scientist series describes the teacher's important role to ensure that children's play and ideas about science are focused, deepened, and challenged. The following examples illustrate the differences between activity-based block study, a thematic approach, and an in-depth exploration of the science of building structures.

Teacher A opens her block area during choice time. A small group of boys uses the area to build roads and play cars. They lay unit blocks end to end for their roads and make a bridge to go over the quicksand. The boys especially enjoy crashing their cars into one another. Later that week, the teacher borrows a play rug printed with roads, signs, and buildings, and lays it down in the block area. The next morning, the boys return to their block area to enjoy "zooming" their cars around the rug's roads. The boys place blocks on different parts of the rug to represent a gas station, their school, and a video store.

In this example, the children actively enjoy playing with the cars and blocks in the block area, but opportunities for both independent and cooperative learning are limited. The cars and blocks stimulate their interest, but there is no guidance or encouragement for them to investigate ideas such as the ways blocks can be stacked and balanced to make garages and bridges, or the physical characteristics of the building materials. Children's interest and curiosity are clear, but the potential for reflection, dialogue, and developing ideas about some interesting and critical physical science concepts is minimal. Moreover, there is little attention paid to the fact that only boys are using the blocks, or to developing strategies to give all children opportunities to build.

Teacher B notices the children's interest in cars and decides to do a project on bridges. She gathers many materials: additional cars and a train set for the block area; books about bridges; a poster of the Golden Gate Bridge; a board game involving train tracks that wind over and under one another on bridges; and a new cityscape puzzle that includes the George Washington Bridge. She plans to use the opportunity to teach the letter *B* to the children as well as the group game London Bridges. The teacher introduces the project with a class discussion asking children to share their experiences with bridges. She identifies the areas in the classroom where there are bridge activities and encourages children to spend some time at each. During the week, she moves through the classroom supporting children's play and, during group time, encourages them to talk about the bridges they've been building for their cars and trains, and share what they've learned about the different kinds and shapes of bridges. Toward the end of the project, the children make a special trip to a train station, take a ride on a train, and count the number of bridges they go over.

In this example, children are surrounded by bridge activities. The block area, the library corner, and the manipulative table have bridge-related activities. The basic literacy, math, and social skills the teacher is focusing on are addressed through these activities. The children are engaged, and visiting the train station and riding on the train are highlights of the week. But this project with its bridge theme has little to do with scientific inquiry and exploration of science concepts.

Teacher C also responds to her children's interest in cars and roads. But she decides that their interest could be the beginning of an exploration of building structures and building materials. When children build roads for their cars, she observes their play and, in the context of their story line, invites them to make multistory parking garages for their vehicles. The next day, she uses a few minutes of group time to show children photographs of the outsides and insides of local parking garages. She also shows them cardboard pieces and roof boards and mentions that she'll be putting them in the block area and at the building center where, ahead of time, she's placed two large boxes of table blocks and a set of small cars. She introduces dollhouse people that will be added to the block area, and three children who haven't shown interest in block play before ask to play there. The children request keeping their roads and garages up overnight so they can continue their play the next day, and she agrees. She also suggests they use the clipboards and paper at the block area to draw their structures, just in case they get knocked down. At the end of the day, the group gathers to share a few memories from the day. The teacher invites one builder to share her problem of adding a third floor to her parking garage, and her solution to stand cylinder blocks in the middle of the second floor to support the third floor.

As in the other examples, children are enjoying playing with the cars and the blocks, but in this case they are engaged in an active, hands-on science inquiry project that illustrates the approach of the Young Scientist series. The teacher builds on the children's interests and has defined a clear set of science concepts to guide their work with blocks. While many other skills are practiced and learned, science is in the foreground.

She focuses the children's attention on important concepts about physical science:

- Forces of gravity, tension, and compression

- Design, stability, and balance

- Characteristics of objects with which children build (such as shape and size)

- Characteristics of materials of which objects are made (such as wood, foam, or plastic)

She encourages deeper thinking to enrich their experiences without interfering in their own process of questioning and exploration. As she does this, the children develop their skills in the following:

- Observing closely
- Raising questions
- Investigating
- Representing things and ideas
- Analyzing

Her questions focus the children's attention on specific designs and strategies they've used to build bridges, and how different blocks respond when used in construction.

As you continue to read this guide and begin to use these techniques, you will learn more about science for young children and what they can do. You will also learn about how to make it possible for children to engage in the rich science exploration exemplified by Teacher C. As you teach, keep in mind these basic principles of the Young Scientist series.

- All three- to five-year-olds can successfully experience rich, in-depth scientific inquiry.

- The content of the science learning draws from children's experiences, is interesting and engaging, and can be explored directly and deeply over time. Expectations are developmentally appropriate; that is, they are realistic and tailored to the strengths, interests, and needs of individual children.

- Discussion, expression, representation, and reflection are critical ways in which children make meaning and develop theories from their active work. Children learn from one another.

- Teachers can take on specific roles and use particular strategies to actively support and guide children's science learning.

Rationale and Goals

Structures are everywhere. Some, such as houses, towers, walls, fences, playground equipment, and billboards, are constructed by people. Others are natural, such as trees, cliffs, and skeletons. Surrounded by structures, it is no surprise that young children are often enthusiastic about building their own.

Many young children have had experiences building either at home or in early childhood settings. Most classrooms provide blocks of different sizes and shapes, as well as additional materials to encourage building and acting out ideas and fantasies. *Building*

Structures, however, will focus children's explorations and deepen their understanding of the physical science present in building.

The specific goals of the exploration are to provide opportunities for children to

- Build with a variety of different materials.

- Experience the ways forces (gravity, compression, tension) affect a structure's stability.

- Build an understanding about how the characteristics of materials affect a structure's stability.

- Develop science inquiry skills including wondering, questioning, exploring and investigating, discussing, reflecting, and formulating ideas and theories.

- Develop scientific dispositions including curiosity, eagerness to find out, an open mind, and delight in being a builder.

The Classroom Environment

One of the most important roles you play in this exploration is to create an environment and culture in your classroom that supports and encourages children's building—the classroom must convey the excitement, challenge, and wonder of building with many different materials. Some of the characteristics of such an environment and culture follow.

THE IMPORTANCE OF BUILDING

A building environment conveys the importance of building structures of all kinds. By providing many kinds of blocks (made from wood, foam, and plastic) and other building materials (such as clay, cardboard, and wire), you create a building environment that challenges children to build in different ways. In the building environment, there is enough space and time to build complicated structures and even leave them standing for further discussion and work. Pictures of buildings and blueprints on the walls and books about buildings placed around the classroom provide children with images of different structures and their characteristics. This importance is also conveyed on walks around the neighborhood as you notice buildings and other structures, and discuss how and of what they are made.

AN EMPHASIS ON INQUIRY

Builders ask questions, observe closely over time, and think about what their observations tell them. What are the special characteristics of the building they are trying to make? What materials would best suit this building project? How can they make a building that is strong enough to house their dinosaurs? A building environment encourages such questions and ideas as well as opportunities for figuring them out.

SHARING OBSERVATIONS AND IDEAS

In a building culture, children are encouraged to share their building experiences and ideas through small and large group discussions, and they learn to listen to what others have to say. They share their records of what they built; their ideas about science concepts, such as what makes a tower stable; and how different kinds of building materials affect a structure's integrity. They learn that ideas are valued and important whether right or wrong; that people may have different ideas; and that one can learn by asking questions of others. They also learn that they need to share how and why they know what they know as well as what they know.

DOCUMENTING AND RECORDING OBSERVATIONS AND IDEAS

Builders spend a great deal of time representing and documenting what they do—using careful sketches and descriptive words to most accurately remember their experiences and share what they have noticed and learned from their explorations. Some builders begin to use drawings to help them plan too. Builders can begin to develop these skills no matter their level of development. In a building environment, materials for representation are easily available and children's work is used to discuss their ideas and stimulate more focused investigations.

Children as Builders

This exploration is designed to provide experiences over time in which children can engage in multiple ways depending on who they are and what they bring. You may find that some children are immediately drawn into the exploration, using everything you set out. Other children may be more reluctant, shying away from the building materials. Some children will quickly grasp the ideas and strategies for building towers and enclosures, while others struggle with these ideas. How children approach this exploration, and what they learn, is influenced by a range of factors including their different developmental levels, experiences, needs, skills, and ideas. As you prepare for this exploration, you will need to consider these factors.

PRIOR EXPERIENCES

Young children bring to an exploration of building their own ideas, interests, and beliefs based in experience and culture, and tempered by their developmental level. Some children may have had more opportunity to play and build with blocks and other materials both indoors and out; others may have had less opportunity. You might find that some of your girls avoid the block area and need specific encouragement to build. Table blocks can be a starting place. Having a time in the block area just for girls or connecting building with the dramatic play area are other possible strategies.

DIVERSE STRENGTHS AND CHALLENGES

Any class presents you with a diverse group of children. All children can explore materials and objects; all children try to make sense of their environment. Each child in your classroom can engage with science and contribute to the classroom learning whether she is three or five years old, speaks English or Spanish or Creole at home, is typically developing or has a special need.

The *Building Structures* exploration relies heavily on children's hands-on building experiences. Be sure that all children, including those with disabilities, have opportunities to observe and explore building structures. As you plan, consider environmental adaptations you may need to make (such as how to arrange the space and how to place the materials so that all children know where to find them and can access them easily). Also think about curriculum adaptations (such as using visual cues or body language to convey information to children whose first language is not English) and materials adaptations (such as having blocks on a table if a child cannot be on the floor) that can support children's participation. Remember that some children may have little experience engaging in play, either alone or with others, and may need you to model and encourage.

COMMUNICATION SKILLS

As with all science, describing and recording what is planned, what actually happens, what is observed, and what happens next is essential. Children will have varying levels of observation, language, and representational skills depending on experience and developmental level. Some children may not have the use of many words to describe what they see but may use their bodies and actions instead. Others may draw with great detail. The drawings of others may only include one major characteristic of a building; for example, a line may represent a tower, or a box may represent a block. In each case, an important characteristic of the building guides the representation. Some children will document what they see using three-dimensional materials. It is important to encourage thinking and representation without expecting or pushing children to go beyond their capabilities.

CHILDREN'S IDEAS

Through their explorations, children will experience the force of gravity pulling their buildings down and the design challenges of building different kinds of structures with different kinds of materials. As you observe children's block building, you will notice responses, both behavioral and verbal, that may provide a window into their thoughts and ideas. You will also notice the building strategies they use. As children place blocks one on top of the other, they may instinctively balance each block. If they see it begin to fall, they may try another way. In the early stages of building, knocking a building down (theirs, not those of others) is part of the learning as well.

Given a variety of different materials, children will become skilled at selecting those they need to do what they want. They may find that the unit block cylinders are the best for building a tall tower. They may discover that the squishiness of foam blocks is a problem if they want to put heavy weight on a building, but that the lightness of the blocks is perfect to build the top of a tower. They may find that straws and connectors make good towers because they are light and long, but if the structure gets too high, it tips or pulls apart when more weight is added. They are likely to choose waffle blocks when they want to build a house big enough to get into because the joints interlock and keep the blocks from pulling apart. Through conversation, questions, and gentle probing, some children will come to new understandings about structures and the forces involved. Other children will need repeated exposure to ideas and experiences over extended periods of time to let go of old ideas and begin to refine and deepen their understanding.

The questions children have also may be very different from the ones you have. You cannot know what every child in your group is thinking, but you may get an idea of different children's points of view by listening to, questioning, and observing children as they explore. It also is helpful to think about some of the typical ideas, questions, and naïve conceptions young children have about some of the basic science concepts that are related to this exploration. You will find information about some of the more common ideas children hold in step 1 of the "Getting Ready" section (p. 13).

Science Exploration through Play

Play is fundamental to children's development, and they approach much of what they do through play. Children engage in many kinds of play when building, including dramatic or symbolic play, exploratory play, and constructive play (Eisenberg 2000). Constructive play permeates what children build; they often engage in dramatic and fantasy play with blocks as they build police stations, zoos, castles, and houses. For some children, props such as human figures, animals, or cars will entice them into the building area. Regardless of what children are building, these situations offer opportunities to extend their thinking and building through encouragement and such questions as, "How high do the walls need to be to hold the elephants?" and "How can we make the castle tower very tall?" Some children will find the building process itself intriguing and engage in exploratory play as they try to balance one block on another, figure out which kinds of blocks will make the tallest tower, or work to build a foundation stable enough to hold up a wall.

You will also want to encourage symbolic play in this exploration by asking children to assume the role of construction workers, architects, engineers, or masons. Books, a guest visitor, and props related to these roles give children some of the information and tools they need to create this kind of symbolic play.

Connections between Science Outcomes and Other Domains

As you provide opportunities for children to explore building materials, and guide them in their development of science inquiry skills, you will also see growth in language, literacy, mathematics, and social skills, as well as in children's approaches to learning. The chart that appears in the appendix (pp. 97–103) shows the connections between science inquiry outcomes as we define them in the Young Scientist series and the outcomes of other subject areas taken from the Head Start Child Outcomes Framework.

Mathematics is one of the languages scientists use to record and reflect on their observations and to communicate their ideas to others. Children who are exploring building materials will also become meaningfully involved with mathematics as they build with blocks and other materials. The blocks themselves are of many geometric shapes; as children build with them, they can experience these different shapes. They can also notice relationships between the unit blocks such as how many square blocks they will need to make a wall the length of one long block. They will experience the symmetry often needed to make towers balance and the patterns (such as in a brick wall) that help make structures stable. And, of course, as they build towers and enclosures, there are endless opportunities for measurement. Some children will simply experience these mathematical concepts, others will talk about them, and still others may use them explicitly as they build.

Scientists also communicate with words. As children communicate their findings, participate in discussions, and represent their experiences they are certainly increasing their language and literacy skills. In fact, research suggests that engaging children in rich science experiences provides a context and a purpose for meaningful language and literacy learning. By engaging with science, children build their vocabulary while developing an ability to communicate their ideas. Such a capacity for oral language provides the foundation for all literacy learning. Children also learn about the importance of books as they use them to get ideas about building techniques, materials, and designs. They learn to record their observations, explanations, and ideas about stability by using multiple forms of representation, including drawings, simple graphs, and writing. Such representations provide a visible record that encourages children to reflect on and talk about their theories and what they have discovered.

Science is a social activity. Whether in person or through other means of communication, scientists exchange ideas, build on one another's work, and often collaborate on science investigations. As children pursue their questions about what makes structures stable, they need to work together to compare findings. Together their individual ideas can suggest a bigger picture and new ideas—placing a flat wooden roof board on top of four wobbly unit block walls will often steady the walls. Such collaborative work (that involves sharing materials and ideas) provides children with significant opportunities for developing their social skills.

Making the Most of the Curriculum

Teachers who implement the Young Scientist series will use a specific approach to teaching: a set of strategies that balance the children's rich explorations with some more structured activities. This curriculum and the accompanying tools and resources are designed to support you as you learn to use this approach. As you prepare to implement *Building Structures with Young Children*, we encourage you to focus on four basic aspects of teaching in a way that may be new to you: the science, the physical environment of the classroom, time and scheduling, and the facilitation and guidance of children's learning.

SCIENCE

You do not need to be a scientist to implement this curriculum. But in order to be responsive to children's explorations, you need to recognize and experience the science phenomena children are experiencing. There is no better way to build this understanding than to engage with the science. When you observe a child working to solve her building problem, you will be much better at guiding her if you have had experiences solving your own. When children raise questions about how to build tall towers, your observations and experiences will help you suggest what children might focus on and what you might show them in a book or tell them. You will appreciate the challenge of drawing a block structure if you have tried it yourself. Before introducing *Building Structures with Young Children* to children, take time to be a builder yourself. You will find activities to guide you in step 1 of the "Getting Ready" section on p. 13; this section will also help you understand common ideas children have about the building materials around them.

PHYSICAL ENVIRONMENT

Science for young children is about investigating real things, developing new ideas and theories, and sharing them with others. The richer and more varied the environment is, the richer and more varied the experiences the children will have. In addition, children's exploration will be more independent and sustained if the tools they need are readily available where and when they need them. You will find guidelines for setting up this environment in steps 3 and 4 of the "Getting Ready" section and in the preparation section of each step. Additional ideas are provided in the resources section.

TIME AND SCHEDULING

Scientific inquiry takes time. Finding out how different building materials respond to being stacked and combined requires weeks of choice time. Focused inquiries into the strategies, designs, and materials used to construct tall towers and sturdy enclosures can last for weeks. As children become engaged, you may find the building going on for three or more months, not just the two you anticipated. A typical schedule often does not include regular time periods of forty-five minutes to an hour and yet this is what is needed for groups of children to study something closely. Often the program calls for a new theme or topic weekly or every two weeks, but *Building Structures with Young Children* should go on for two to three months with some observations and activities spread out across the year. Suggestions for scheduling different activities are provided in the "Getting Ready" section and throughout the guide. You will also find suggestions for making extended study possible.

FACILITATING AND GUIDING LEARNING

With your own building exploration under your belt, a physical environment that invites and supports children's inquiry, and a schedule that allows the time, the stage is set for the most important part of teaching—your interactions with the children. There may be some new strategies to learn, new expectations required, and old approaches to let go of. This guide is designed to help you become a teacher of science—engaging children in science and focusing and deepening their experiences and thinking. The step-by-step guide is designed to help you as you learn new roles and approaches.

Involve Families

Families are important to *Building Structures with Young Children*. In cases where parents are not the sole caregivers, you can involve a grandparent, foster parent, aunt, uncle, older sibling, or cousin. As you involve families, consider how culture might influence a child's block play. For example, some families may assume block play is for boys; some families may discourage children from playing with blocks or other open-ended building materials; others may come from cultures where children are expected to listen, not to mess about. Talk with family members to learn about their cultures and children's experiences. This knowledge will help you engage families appropriately and respectfully.

And families have much to share about their children. Individual children may have had interesting or problematic experiences playing with blocks that are important to know. Some children may have built clubhouses, tree houses, or other structures at home. Others may have had a bad experience being bossed around by other builders or criticized for their efforts. They may have relatives who are contractors, carpenters, plumbers, bricklayers, construction laborers, or architects. Families can provide you with important clues about such experiences as well as what building materials intrigue their children, what questions they have, and what strategies you might use to support children's learning.

Take steps at the beginning to inform families about *Building Structures with Young Children*—what you will be doing, what children will learn, and why this is important for children's development. Feel free to use or adapt the sample letter on p. 83 that introduces families to the exploration. If a caregiver does not speak English, find someone to help you translate the letter or make an audiotape in their home language. Also invite families into the classroom or host a family night where families can experience firsthand the importance of your science explorations and experiment with ways to promote children's explorations of structures and building at home and in the community.

Be sure to let families know that their participation is welcome and needed and that you are interested in having them share their expertise as well as their concerns. Family members can be rich resources if they have cultural stories to share, experiences building different kinds of structures, or knowledge about places to visit. Also, encourage family members to work as classroom volunteers. Some families may be able to help in the classroom on a regular basis; others may come in just for special occasions such as field trips or special events. They can serve as invaluable assets when you take the class outdoors, providing children with the adult guidance they need to help them focus and observe more deeply. Indoors, family volunteers can assist with small group explorations and ensure that an environment of respect for buildings and structures is maintained while children's curiosity is promoted.

Let parents know what they can do at home with their children. For example, they might build together. Suggest different building materials and experiences they might share. In addition to blocks, families can build with paper cups and sponges. They might also want to build a fort out of blankets and chairs. Family outings are another great way for children and families to see the science in their communities. Suggest places to go. For example, a trip to a local skyscraper or large auditorium can spark children's curiosity about tall towers and large expansive enclosures. Such activities can reinforce and extend the science children are learning in the classroom, while helping children and families see science phenomena in their daily lives. It is also helpful to provide sample questions that families can use to spark children's thinking and questions. The "Families Building Structures" handout included on p. 84 of the resources section provides families with ideas for activities and thoughtful questions they can ask their children. You might also provide families with a list of children's books that relate to the science concepts they are learning. See the "Books and Web Sites" section (p. 82) for some suggestions.

How to Use This Guide

Building Structures with Young Children includes three stages that will guide you in promoting children's exploration of building materials and structures and their use of inquiry.

GETTING READY. To facilitate this exploration, you will need to prepare. This section will help you to explore the science concepts embedded in this exploration.

This section will also help you prepare the physical environment and think about routines and schedules that support children's inquiry into building structures.

OPEN EXPLORATION. During this stage, children explore a variety of building materials at a number of building centers. These initial explorations are intended to encourage children to find out how they can build with these various building materials. During this stage, children will also look at books and images of different kinds of buildings to inspire their block play. This is the time to encourage children to follow their interests and try things out. Resist the temptation to share your own ideas about balance, stability, and characteristics of materials. Instead, encourage children to follow up on their ideas and try new things.

FOCUSED EXPLORATION. After children have had multiple opportunities to openly explore a variety of building materials, they are ready for focused exploration. During this stage, you encourage children to think more about how the materials and designs they choose make tall towers taller, or enclosures bigger. Your role is to deepen children's understandings by asking probing questions, encouraging children to represent their work, and creating opportunities for discussion and reflection. Extension activities—such as a field trip to a nearby construction site, the sharing of an interesting book or reference material, or a visit from a structural engineer—take place about once a week throughout "Focused Exploration." These experiences motivate children to continue their explorations in new ways, provide new information, and connect their work to their lives outside of school.

"Focused Exploration" includes two different studies. The towers study focuses on helping children look at the ways their choice of building materials, designs, and strategies affect a tall structure's stability. The enclosures study focuses on helping children look at the ways their choice of building materials, designs, and strategies affect the strength of the walls, roofs, stories, and other things they add to their enclosures.

Each step of "Open Exploration" and "Focused Exploration" includes the following sections:

The **CORE EXPERIENCES** provide a rationale for the step—what science ideas you will be focusing on, why this is important for children, and how this step relates to the overall exploration.

The **PREPARATION** section will help you get ready for each step as you consider your classroom schedule, the materials you will need, and ways to connect with families.

The **TEACHING PLAN** offers detailed guidance for implementing the step, including what you might say and do to engage children and facilitate their explorations and help them reflect on their experiences and ideas. The left-hand column of this section guides you through the exploration. Issues teachers have raised and our responses are found in the right-hand column, which also includes photographs, drawings, and sample dialogue. This column gives you a picture of what the plan looks like "in action," while suggesting ways to extend science explorations.

The teaching plan is composed of three consecutive parts: Engage, Explore, and Reflect. Engage offers suggestions for what you might say and do to encourage children to get excited about and involved in building structures. Explore offers guidance for what you can do to facilitate their explorations. Reflect suggests different ways to use representation and discussion to help children reflect on their experiences and developing ideas.

At the end of the section on open exploration, you will find three different types of extensions for enriching children's building explorations. They include planning a field trip to explore different structures or a construction site, inviting experts into the classroom, and using books and videos to extend the exploration.

The resource section provides more information about the teaching approach of *Building Structures with Young Children*, essential information for working with buildings and structures; and book and Web resources. We encourage you to familiarize yourself with this section before you start. You will find references to the resources throughout the guide. Some of what is there may be useful to you right away; other material may be more helpful after you have had some initial experiences teaching *Building Structures with Young Children*.

Building High: Excerpts from a Teacher's Journal

These journal entries illustrate what one Head Start teacher learned when she helped her children in becoming young builders.

SEPTEMBER 14

It's hard to believe that next week I'll have twenty children in my classroom! This year I plan to make the block area a more important place for kids' science learning.

I've already spent an afternoon exploring some of the open-ended building materials myself. I've had these materials in my classroom for years but never really thought about how they can be used to build, which ones are better for what, how to make stronger or taller structures, and much more.

I've also been working on my room. So far I've been able to make my block area almost twice the normal size. Somehow, making it bigger makes the whole area more important. I have a stash of building materials—unit blocks, foam squares and circles, and waffle blocks—as well as space for both hard and soft building surfaces. There's even room for a "Do Not Touch" table so kids can save their structures, and there's a table with clipboards and markers so kids can draw pictures of their structures. And I found some posters—one of Los Angeles at night and one of Paris. I found some great books at the library with pictures of interesting structures and stories about building. I have displayed many of these on top of the block shelves so the children can easily refer to them while working.

I guess what I'm really trying to do is develop a classroom culture—a classroom environment that yells *build*.

OCTOBER 6

I feel like I'm really getting to know the kids and their families. As for the building theme . . . I got stuck. At first, the kids were really drawn to the blocks—how could they not be? But for a while, most of the fun was in knocking down the stacks they built up. So I've been trying to figure out how to focus the kids again on the building.

But I think I made a breakthrough. Just the other day I happened to sit in the block area during choice time. For a while I just observed, and somehow I think that my being there signaled to the kids that I was interested in what they were doing—that their play was important.

And I learned from watching them—seeing what was getting in their way, what their points of frustration were, and what they were trying to do. Alina, for example, kept placing one block on top of another, then one on top, across the two, like a doorway. After watching her try this for a while, I said that I noticed that the top block kept rolling off. She then got three of the long wooden cylinder blocks and tried to do the same thing. I think she understood that she needed to try different blocks but was unaware of the properties she needed to consider. This time the top cylinder rolled off, so I wondered out loud what would happen if she used a different block for the top piece.

Her response was to try a different kind of block for the top, and this time it worked! Then Reuben came over and began to copy Alina's explorations, beginning with the foam blocks. I'm beginning to see more clearly how the materials I present guide children's science explorations.

OCTOBER 18

There are towers everywhere and kids are building towers with any kind of material they can get their hands on—cardboard blocks, foam cylinders, wooden cylinders, and unit blocks.

Today as I watched Reuben, Alina, and Joy building, I decided it was time to give them a challenge. So I pulled out some unit blocks, foam squares, and circles and asked which they thought they could use to build the tallest tower. I guess I was trying to help them think about the different materials—their properties, their limitations, and their possibilities. They really took up the challenge, trying to figure out what materials and strategies work best for building high. And now they're building even higher!

OCTOBER 24

Today during group time we talked about towers and what it takes to build high. Here are some of their ideas:

- You have to put the blocks right on top of the other block.
- The tower stands up better if you build it on the roof-board blocks instead of the rug.
- Sometimes you have to move the blocks back and forth so the tower will stop tipping.
- Sometimes you have to take some blocks off.
- The tower will stand up better if you put some more blocks right next to the tower to help hold it up.

I wrote these ideas down. They will make a great documentation panel along with the pictures I took.

OCTOBER 30

Kids keep building towers. Some kids built straight up. Kenya had a real design going and still got tall. Joy decided to build a brace. Miguel's was the simplest but the tallest.

And ever since I hung journals next to the blocks, kids have been drawing their towers too. Today they drew their structures from a couple different angles. They are working on drawing the exact shapes of the blocks they have used. We also started thinking of ways to measure their towers. I used the digital camera for the first time, which was neat because the kids could see everything from a different perspective right away. (Miguel could see how tall his tower was compared with his own height!)

NOVEMBER 15

Today Kenya, Avi, and Chris built a tower of large cylinder blocks. It was so tall they had to stand on chairs, trying to hold the tower to keep it up. When they asked me for help, I said that we needed to figure out why it won't stand up. After a few minutes, they balanced it, and it stood by itself.

When I asked how tall their building was, they got the poster of Miguel's tower. In the poster, the tower goes up to Miguel's mouth. So then they needed Miguel. Mia got him and asked him to stand next to the new tower. It came up to his shoulder. "So his is bigger," said Mia. But Chris can't believe it. He says, "Prove it." So Avi counts the blocks. He discovers that the photo tower has thirteen unit blocks. The new tower has eleven.

So this building stuff leads to new investigations—it's like new doors keep opening. In a way, it's about being there and really hearing kids' questions to figure out what they are working on and what they are trying to figure out. So what they need from me are the materials to work with, some guidance on method, the mechanics of how to systematize their explorations, and help documenting their discoveries.

REFERENCES

Carson, Rachel. 1965. *The sense of wonder.* New York: Harper & Row.

Eisenberg, M. 2000. The influence of materials on children's play: Explorations at the water table. Unpublished study, Tufts University.

National Research Council. 1996. *National science education standards.* Washington, D.C.: National Academy Press.

getting ready

Step 1: Preparing Yourself—Science

You may have spent hours building structures as a child. And as a teacher, you probably have spent some time helping children as they build. But when was the last time you had a chance to really sit down and experiment using different types of materials to create your own structures? Even if you have had few building experiences, you can use this section to develop the basic understandings that prepare you for helping children explore the science behind building. All you need are walking shoes, a clipboard with paper and pencils, some building materials (unit blocks, small-scale table blocks, straws and connectors, and some foam or waffle blocks), and a willingness to explore and wonder. (For more information about the different building materials you need, refer to step 3 below, "Preparing the Physical Environment—Materials and Resources" on p. 16.)

TEACHING PLAN

Take a walk through the neighborhood and bring along a clipboard with paper and one or two pencils. Look at buildings, signposts, billboards, and more. If you know of a structure that's in the process of being built, check it out. Notice the way that walls are built, the way that building materials (such as bricks, wood, steel girders, and so on) are laid, how signs and poles stand up, and the shapes in the structure (triangles, squares, rectangles, circles). As you observe, take some time to sketch the structures you see, trying to capture some of their details.

When you return to the classroom, try re-creating some things you saw on your walk with the building materials you have available, using your sketches for reference.

First, think about the walls you examined and the way the materials were laid. Try building a block wall in the same style. Do walls made of rows of blocks that are stacked one on top of the other fall more easily than walls that are built with the blocks overlapping from row to row?

Now think about the signs and poles you saw. Try to make a pencil stand up on end. What do you need to do to make it stable? Do you

> **TEACHER NOTE:** When I took a walk around the neighborhood today, it struck me how many buildings are made of brick. Then I started making sketches of the buildings, and I began to see a pattern in the way that bricks are laid out. I mean, the bricks are never laid out one exactly on top of another, and the rows of bricks always overlap. So now I'm starting to wonder if it's just to make the buildings look nice—or is it really about stability?

find that you need a base in order to keep it standing up? What do you think keeps signposts and telephone poles from falling over?

And what about the shapes in the structures you saw? Try building a structure with straws and connectors. Make a square and a triangle. Do you find that the triangles are stronger than the squares? The supporting frameworks of many structures have triangles in them. In other structures, the joints are so strong that triangles aren't needed.

Continue building in order to become familiar with the other materials children will use and confront the different building challenges they will face.

Build different towers out of unit blocks. Look for the following:

- The way you need to place the blocks to make the strongest tower. Try stacking them on their ends, on their thin sides, and on their wide sides. Which ones are most stable? Which are strongest? Try using the cylinders. What do you think makes some towers stronger than others?

- The strength of towers that are more than one block wide. Build a tower with the blocks directly on top of one another and then try a tower where the blocks overlap. Do you find that making the base broader makes your tower more stable? Do you find that if your blocks are overlapped like bricks, the tower is stronger? Why do you think this is true?

Build different towers with Kapla or other small-scale table blocks. Look for the following:

- The differences in skinny towers, fat towers, and towers with strong foundations.

- The strength and stability of a tower that has space inside.

- Towers that are not symmetrical or straight up and down.

Try building towers that are more complex. How can you make pieces stick out? Can you build doors and windows? What do you need to do to make uneven-shaped towers stable?

Build different towers with straws and connectors. Look for the following:

- New challenges these materials present; for example, try building high. Is your tower tall but unsteady? Straws are not very stable because they are so light.

- Strengths and weaknesses of straw buildings. Try putting or hanging things on your tower; the straws may bend or tip. They are good for building up but not very strong. What happens if you make some triangles? Will it make your tower stronger?

Experiment with foam or waffle blocks. Look for special features of these materials.

- Can you build towers with them? Are they better for other types of building? Are towers made out of foam as strong and as stable?

TEACHER NOTE: I really didn't think I wanted to spend time exploring the building materials, but once I got started I really got into it! I found it very helpful to have questions in mind as I worked ... suddenly my exploration felt like science.

TEACHER NOTE: I made a quick sketch of my unit block tower and when I looked at it, I noticed how the whole top section looked especially wobbly. No wonder! It took me about five minutes to balance that part on the two thin supports.

Build different enclosures or houses with unit blocks and small-scale table blocks. Look for the following:

- Design. Try building a house. You will need to think about walls and how they stand up. Enclosures will often need a roof. How will it stand up? You may find that if the roof is light, it will need less support but may be less strong. How can you support a heavier roof? What design seems to be the most stable?

- Windows and doors. Windows and doors present special challenges. How can you design them so that the building remains strong?

- New challenges. What challenges do you experience? How are these challenges different from the ones you experience when building a tower? How are they the same?

Build different enclosures with straws and connectors, considering:

- Design. Make a frame for a house out of straws. How would you make walls and a roof? The straw frame must hold up the walls and roof. How can you make it strong?

- Framework. Straw structures resemble scaffolding or the framework of a house. How does your framework compare with what you have seen outdoors?

Build different enclosures with foam or waffle blocks. Notice and think about design. Given the properties of these blocks, what is easier or harder to do?

Sketch one or two of the structures you have built. Consider how sketching or drawing the structure before building helped you to pay more careful attention to its design. What new features did you notice?

Now that you have used different materials to build a variety of structures, you have explored some of the science concepts children will likely experience as they engage in *Building Structures*. Learning a bit more about these concepts will help you recognize the science embedded in children's building. The information that follows is not intended for young children; it is to guide your work with them. Children can only develop an understanding of these concepts as they explore selected materials and process their experiences with you as their guide.

- *Forces: gravity, tension, and compression*
  Gravity is the attraction that objects exert on one another. The force between the earth and other objects is strong because the earth is so big. Structures have to be built so that they resist the pull of gravity and stand up. Some parts of a structure are pressed and squeezed together. That force is called *compression*. Other parts are pulled apart. That force is called *tension*. If you push down on a triangle made of Tinker Toys, the sidepieces are being compressed whereas the bottom one is under tension.

- *Certain designs make structures stronger and more stable*
  A structure has to be designed so that it counteracts the force of gravity. It must be built so it is balanced and the forces on it are in equilibrium; otherwise it will tip or collapse or parts will break. It must be built with a strong enough foundation and a relatively low center of gravity so it doesn't collapse under its own weight or tip easily.

- *Different building materials have different characteristics depending on what they are made of and how they are made*
  Some can be pulled hard before they break; some are flexible and bend; others can have a lot of weight put on them without breaking. Things you build with also can be of different sizes, shapes, and textures. The characteristics of building materials are important to consider when designing and building structures.

Step 2: Preparing Yourself—The Guide

This teacher's guide is an important tool for you. It offers detailed, step-by-step guidance on how to prepare and implement each step. Read it through before you begin.

TEACHING PLAN

Read the guide carefully. It will help you understand the science focus of each step as well as the various roles you can take to guide children's inquiry.

The teaching plan offers detailed guidance for implementing each step, including what you might say and do. Issues teachers have raised with responses, as well as photographs, drawings, and sample dialogue provide pictures of what the plan looks like "in action."

Step 3: Preparing the Physical Environment—Materials and Resources

Children's learning and excitement will be heightened by the variety and quality of the materials they are able to explore. Gathering these materials now will help you to provide children with rich opportunities for exploration.

In this step you will

- Collect building materials that vary in size, shape, weight, texture, degrees of flexibility, and what they are made of.

- Collect art materials that can be used to represent structures in a variety of forms.

- Collect building-related books, videos, posters, and photos.

TEACHER NOTE: Because we had never done this curriculum before, another teacher and I spent an afternoon going through it. Together, we figured out what materials we would need, what our goals would be, what we expected kids to do, and how our own roles would change over time. Going through the guide together helped us to talk through our questions too.

ISSUE: *What if we don't have all these materials?*

RESPONSE: Many of these materials are costly, and programs cannot be expected to purchase them all. However, the amount and quality of the materials you make available to children will determine the kinds of building in which children will engage, so do all you can. One strategy would be to borrow the materials from other classrooms, and then lend yours to those classrooms when you have finished the exploration. Remember, too, that a variety of building materials can be found at recycle centers, and some can be collected from builders.

TEACHING PLAN

1. Collect as many of the following building materials as possible. Make sure you have enough of these materials to allow four or five children to use any one of the materials at the same time. Many building materials can be made or purchased cheaply. The numbers in parentheses are suggested amounts for up to five children. You may need to borrow materials from other classrooms.

- Unit blocks (150–200): roof boards, quadruple units, and additional large cylinder blocks have proved to be popular
- Cardboard blocks (40–50)
- Three different types of small-scale table blocks (150–200 blocks per set; see the resources section, p. 81, for suggestions)
- Straws and connectors (at least 100)
- Pieces of oaktag, cardboard, or matte board (letter size and larger)
- Foam blocks (40–50)
- Small boxes or cardboard milk cartons, some filled with sand and taped shut
- Scraps of wood from a carpenter or a lumber store
- Coffee stirrers and clay

2. Collect as many of the following art, drawing, and writing materials as possible. Borrow materials from other classrooms, if necessary.

- Markers, both fat and thin
- Crayons and pencils
- Paper in a variety of sizes
- Paints
- Clay or plasticine
- Small pieces of foam, scraps of wood, and scraps of cardboard—salvaged or recycled
- Clipboards (6) (Options include full-size clipboards or cardboard with a bulldog clip attached.)
- Pencils, ideally attached to the clipboards by Velcro or string (Some classes might prefer shorter, stubbier writing implements.)

3. Collect props that encourage children to build as part of their dramatic play. Look for the following:

- Toy road signs
- Trees
- Vehicles
- Animals
- People

ISSUE: *What about building materials that stick together such as Legos and Duplos?*

RESPONSE: These kinds of materials are great, but they serve different purposes. Because they stick together, these materials do not focus children's attention directly on balance, symmetry, and construction strategies.

ISSUE: *A lot of the books with good pictures of structures are written for much older kids.*

RESPONSE: Young children enjoy looking at pictures in all sorts of books. There's no need to worry about the writing style if the pictures are engaging. After all, these pictures can serve as inspiration for children's building.

4. Collect other building-related resources, such as these:

- Books or posters about construction

- Pictures of different structures and buildings in process, as well as pictures of bridges, playground equipment, scaffolding, and so on

See "Books and Web Sites" (p. 82) for suggestions.

Step 4: Preparing the Physical Environment—Classroom Set-Up

You have taken time to collect a variety of materials that children will be excited to explore. To get the most out of these materials, you need to create a classroom environment that supports and motivates children's building.

TEACHING PLAN

1. Organize your classroom to provide children with the following:

- A block area that easily accommodates four or five builders. Place blocks on shelves so children have easy access. Label shelves with cutout shapes of each type of unit block so children can put blocks away independently.

- At least two additional areas (building centers) in the classroom where small groups of children can explore small-scale table blocks, such as Kapla or cube blocks. These building centers provide even more opportunities for children to engage with a range of building materials. When thinking about areas in your classroom for these building centers, choose tables or floor areas that have plenty of flat surfaces and are not in the middle of classroom traffic.

- Shelves for art and writing materials that are placed so children can get supplies easily. Label these shelves so children can put away supplies independently.

2. Organize your classroom display spaces to provide children with the following:

- Wall space at their eye level on which to hang their drawings and paintings, as well as pictures or posters of interesting structures

- A shelf, at the children's eye level, to display the three-dimensional representations children make of their structures, such as collages, clay sculptures, and smaller block structures

- Access to a selection of books related to structures (See "Books and Web Sites" on p. 82.)

3. Plan to borrow building materials, if necessary, so children will be able to build with enough different materials. See p. 81 for

---

TEACHER NOTE: Because my children speak so many different languages, I decided to post pictures of buildings from the many different parts of the world their families come from.

TEACHER NOTE: I've been working on my room. So far I've been able to make my block area almost twice the normal size. Somehow, making it bigger makes the whole area seem more important.

ISSUE: *How will I find space?*

RESPONSE: We know it is difficult to find extra space in any classroom. For this exploration, you will need to clear whatever surfaces, shelves, and bulletin boards you can. It may also be necessary to simply put some things away. Teachers have found that children become involved in the explorations when many areas of the classroom invite children to build.

ISSUE: *I have no wall space.*

RESPONSE: It is important for children to see their work, photos, and documentation panels. (See p. 92 for information on documentation panels.) Try using backs of cupboards and doors, or use a large piece of cardboard as a portable bulletin board.

guidance on kinds and numbers of materials for children's building exploration.

4. Plan to spend at least a week enlarging your block area, setting up your classroom space as described above in step 3, and exploring the building materials as described in step 1, p. 13.

Step 5: Classroom Schedule and Routines

Building Structures with Young Children is not a theme or activity-based curriculum but a science inquiry that develops over time. It does not assume that all children spend all of their time building. Your children will have time to engage in play and reflection that are not building-focused, even as the *Building Structures with Young Children* inquiry continues. The more time children have to explore a variety of building materials and reflect on their experiences, however, the more they will get out of the study. In addition, be sure you have one or two building centers open, along with the block area, which increases the number of opportunities children have for engaging in the exploration.

TEACHING PLAN

1. Review your weekly schedule. Make time for the following:

   • 5–10 minutes before each choice time to prepare children for the day's exploration

   • 30–45 minutes of choice time, at least four times per week

   • 10–15 minutes for a meeting with the whole group, at least once per week

2. Review your long-range schedule. Anticipate that the exploration could last for more than a month.

   • Open exploration can last from a few weeks to two months.

   • Focused exploration of towers can come before, after, or at the same time as the focus on enclosures. It will likely last three weeks or longer, depending on children's interests.

   • Focused exploration of enclosures can come before, after, or at the same time as the focus on towers. It, too, will likely last three weeks or longer, depending on children's interests.

   • Children's interest in block play will continue even after the building structures exploration has finished.

3. Review your routines and safety procedures for block building. If they are too restrictive, children will be limited in their explorations of towers and other structures.

   • If possible, allow children to return to their block building for a few consecutive days during the week.

We use the term *choice time* to mean the time during the day when children are working in small groups or individually on a variety of activities. Some people call this time *activity time, center time, play time,* or *work time.*

ISSUE: *I rotate my children through the block area during the week. How can I allow some of them to play in an area two or three days in a row?*

RESPONSE: You might make a new classroom rule that allows a group of children to return to the block area or a building center every day for a week before you give other children a turn to do the same.

- Consider ways, if possible, to allow block structures to stay standing from one day to the next so children have the opportunity to sustain a building project. You might have children make "please save" signs for their structures. Try rearranging you room so there's enough room for nap cots without having to use the block area.

- Consider allowing children to build over their heads and providing hard hats for them to wear and stable chairs or stools for them to stand on if they need to add blocks to tall structures.

4. Be prepared to observe children's block play and record what you notice.

- Schedule times when you can observe children's block play for ten minutes, two or three times a week. During this time, plan activities where other children can work independently in other areas of the room. You might also ask your co-teacher, assistant, or volunteer to manage the other areas of the room during this time.

- Read the observation and assessment section (p. 77). Prepare a clipboard so you can easily record your observations of children's building explorations.

Step 6: Families

Children may have already had opportunities to play and build with blocks by the time they begin your class. Connecting with families from the start will allow you to build on children's life experiences and use family resources. It will also help you build a partnership with families with the goal of engaging their children in science inquiry.

TEACHING PLAN

Send a letter to families that describes the important science understandings children will develop as they focus on building with blocks and other materials, and suggest ways that families can support children's science learning. There is a sample letter to families on p. 83 in the resource section; you can copy or adapt it to fit your circumstances and your families.

- Find out who might volunteer or who has skills and building experience (such as masons, builders, and architects) to share with the class.

- Invite families to build together in the classroom once or twice during the study.

- Set up a bulletin board where family members can see examples of their children's work.

ISSUE: *Where do I get hard hats?*

RESPONSE: We've found that the play hard hats sold as props for construction dramatic play are fine. Some teachers also use the dramatic play firefighter hats.

ISSUE: *I don't have time to observe children's block play.*

RESPONSE: Consider observing children's block play as part of your teaching time. It is just as important as working with children on letter recognition activities at a table, for example. The information you get from your observations is very important for planning for and scaffolding children's science inquiry.

TEACHER NOTE: When Phil came in and showed how he makes blueprints, the kids were really excited. A number of them actually drew their own plans before they started building.

open exploration

Most three- to five-year-olds have some experience playing with blocks, but some have not. These initial experiences along with a good and varied supply of building materials will provide all children with the opportunity to explore different blocks as part of their play, in a number of different classroom building centers. As children get to know what they can build with different kinds of building materials, and they begin to notice how different blocks of different shapes, sizes, texture, and density differ, teachers have opportunities to observe their play, looking for ways to acknowledge and support their open exploration.

Step 1: Introduce Children to Building Structures

This initial step helps you set the tone for an exciting and manageable exploration of building structures. It guides your thoughtful introduction of new materials, rules, and routines, and it introduces you to some of the strategies and roles you will be using throughout *Building Structures*.

CORE EXPERIENCES

☐ Share prior building experiences.

☐ Hear about building materials in various building centers.

☐ Explore building materials.

☐ Share current building experiences.

PREPARATION

☐ Display books about structures in the block area and building centers.

☐ Hang posters of structures, including enlarged photos of local buildings.

☐ Read the section on science teaching (pp.4–6) for information about young children's inquiry and for strategies you can use to engage children in the exploration.

SCHEDULE

Set the schedule for the duration of a week, or until all children have had a chance to build with different materials.

☐ 5–10 minutes for whole group meeting to introduce the exploration

☐ 45–60 minutes for choice times, four or five times per week

☐ 5–10 minutes for whole-group discussion

MATERIALS

Block area:

☐ Unit blocks

Building centers:

☐ Kapla or Dr. Drew blocks

☐ Foam blocks

☐ Camera, if possible

☐ Copy of the observation record form (p. 93)

☐ Charts: "What We Made with Blocks" and "Building Guidelines"

FAMILY CONNECTION

☐ Send home a note that introduces the "Building Structures" study and that suggests ways families might help. (See p. 83 for sample letter.)

☐ Schedule and plan an evening when parents and other family members can meet in the classroom, build with the various materials, and talk about ways you can work together to support the study in and out of school.

TEACHING PLAN

ENGAGE

Lead a discussion with a large group before children's first open exploration: five to ten minutes is plenty.

ISSUE: *My children have already built a lot with blocks. Why should I introduce them again?*

RESPONSE: It is true that blocks will not be new to many children. But the focus of this exploration is not on the blocks themselves, but on building and the characteristics of strong, stable structures. Looking at these familiar materials in this way will help children begin to focus on the science of building with blocks.

This teacher was careful to include images as well as children's words.

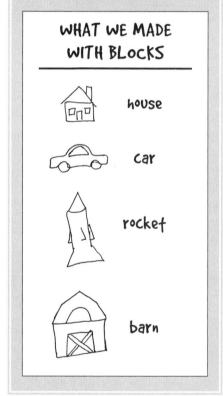

WHAT WE MADE WITH BLOCKS

house

car

rocket

barn

Discuss children's prior experiences with blocks and other building materials.

When you start the exploration, gather the children together in a circle. If your block area is large enough, gather the group there. Point out the other building centers, and begin a discussion about children's prior experiences with blocks and other building materials. Use questions like these:

- *What do you like to build out of blocks? Can you tell us about it?*
- *What did it look like?*
- *What kind of blocks do you like to use? Why?*

Ask follow-up questions, and invite other children to participate:

- *Dylan, when you made your barn, what kind of walls did you build?*
- *How did the horses get in and out of your barn?*
- *Tabitha, how did you get the people in and out of the house you built?*
- *How did they get upstairs?*

Record children's ideas on the chart labeled "What We Made with Blocks." Include images as well as children's words.

Discuss rules for builders.

Tell children that they will have many opportunities to build wonderful structures in the block area and in the building centers. Include children in developing classroom expectations and routines for using, moving, and putting blocks away. You might say the following:

- *Show us a safe way to take blocks off the shelves.*
- *Show us a safe way to take a structure apart without knocking it over.*
- *Show us how you can put unit blocks away safely.*

Describe these expectations and routines on the chart labeled "Building Guidelines." Include rules that you and the children decide might help them build safely at the building centers such as the following:

- *If blocks fall onto the floor, pick them up and put them back on the table.*

Post the "Building Guidelines" chart and plan to reinforce the rules with children as they play.

SAMPLE GUIDELINES FOR SAFE AND FUN BLOCK PLAY

- Blocks are for building.
- Take blocks off the shelves as you need them.
- Take structures apart from the top and go down.
- Don't crash the blocks.
- Don't throw the blocks.
- Don't walk on the blocks.
- Push a small pile of blocks to the shelves and then put them where they belong.

TEACHER NOTE: I used part of morning meeting to demonstrate safe ways to move hollow blocks.

ISSUE: *I don't trust my children to come up with appropriate guidelines.*

RESPONSE: When you take children's suggestions seriously, they tend to rise to the occasion. If a child suggests a rule that seems silly or unrealistic, genuinely try to find out the thinking behind their suggestion. As children explain their thinking, they tend to reassess unrealistic ideas about rules and reframe them as reasonable ones.

EXPLORE

Throughout the first week, observe and acknowledge children's block play.

Observe and document children's block play.

As children explore, notice how they use the materials. Some will build a "thing" and others will build simply to find out what the materials do. Use the observation form to record what children say and do, using these questions as a guide.

- What are they building?
- Which children are involved?
- Are children choosing to explore alone or with peers?
- Are they placing the blocks flat on surfaces and building things like roads?
- Are they stacking blocks one on top of the other?
- Are they making bridges by placing blocks horizontally across vertical supports?

Use the following suggestions to help you document the children's work with the blocks:

- Take photographs or make sketches of the structures children build.
- Write down the questions children ask and the comments they make related to their buildings.
- Use the observation record forms to document what children say and do.

You will need this information to lead a conversation with the whole group at the end of the week.

Children's Names	Seen and Heard
Shirley	• uses Kapla flat and on sides • "It's a pool! See the diving board?" • many sided, flat and not up
Julia	• hollow block baby's bed • enclosure, no roof • some blocks on their sides—others flat

ISSUE: *I know it's important to observe children's block play during choice time, but I'm pulled in so many directions. What can I do?*

RESPONSE: During some of your choice time, try planning activities where most of the children can play independently in different areas of the room, allowing you to focus your attention on the children doing science. Volunteers can also help other children.

Acknowledge children's block play.

Acknowledge children's block play with a smile. Engaged builders can be left to explore while you observe. Observing children's block play gives them a clear message that you value and acknowledge what they are doing.

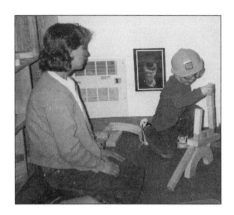

Some children will invite you to look at their structures. Ask them to talk about the buildings, and then consider introducing building vocabulary with comments like the following:

- *Your house has an upstairs and a downstairs!*
- *You've used these rectangular blocks for the foundation and the square ones for the walls.*

Use follow-up questions to extend your conversation:

- *Have you ever seen a building like this one? Where? Who used it?*
- *How is yours different?*

TEACHER NOTE: I used to think I needed to be interacting with children to be teaching them. Now I realize how much I learn about them by observing their play.

ISSUE: *My children need me to interact with them or they won't build.*

RESPONSE: Explain to your builders that you are in the block area to watch them build instead of talking or building with them. Some teachers put a special hat or name tag on when they are observing so their children can learn to understand the special role.

TEACHER NOTE: The children in my inclusion class are enjoying open exploration! Those with sensory issues enjoy the quietness of the foam blocks. And the two children with motor issues are using the blocks that have velcro stuck to them, and so are the other children! It's wonderful to see them building together. With adult support and encouragement, some are able to manipulate the smaller blocks too. My child who has muscular dystrophy has trouble grasping the unit blocks, so he's found friends to build with who put blocks where he wants them. And my child with pervasive developmental disorder didn't build with his friends until just yesterday. I was reminded that he needs an initial period of playing by himself and observing others.

REFLECT

At the end of the week, discuss children's exploration of blocks with the whole group for five to ten minutes.

Share experiences.

Gather your whole group together in a circle. Share an observation you made of a child solving a building problem or a photograph of a child's structure. Initiate a conversation with comments and questions such as the following:

- *Iris, I drew this picture of the palace you built. Can you tell your friends what you did?*

- *Remember when it started to fall? Tell us what you did then.*

- *Oliver used the small blocks to make this rocket. He was able to save it on this clipboard for you all to see. Oliver, tell us about your rocket.*

- *Do you remember when you rebuilt it here at the bottom? How did you change it?*

Review the building guidelines.

Allow a few minutes during a meeting with the whole group to comment on the successful ways children have been using the building materials. For example, you might say:

- *When it was time for Ramos and Miguel to take apart their elevator yesterday, I noticed how carefully they took blocks from the top and put them away on the shelves. Can you two show us how you did that?*

TEACHER NOTE: I held up the photograph I took of Isha's truck. After she told us about where the driver sits, I asked her to tell us about building the truck's roof.

Isha: *It fell.*

Teacher: *How did you get it to stay up?*

Isha: *I use two.*

Teacher: *Oh, I see! Over on this side there are two blocks holding the roof up. Why do you think that helps?*

Isha: *It's strong.*

EXAMPLE: This teacher brought a block area problem to the group and asked them to help her solve it.

Teacher: *I've noticed how long it takes us to put the unit blocks away at the end of choice time. Can you help me think of a way we can get more children to help put the blocks back on the shelves?*

Child 1: *The kids that play there need to clean up there.*

Teacher: *So we could remind the children who play in the block area that they'll be responsible for putting the blocks away?*

Child 2: *There's so many blocks.*

Teacher: *You'd like help putting the blocks away?*

Child 2: *Yup.*

Child 1: *You're allowed to ask for help. That'll be the rule.*

Also, discuss any issues that may be interfering with children's block play.

- *I've noticed some of you taking all of the blocks off the shelves as soon as you get into the block area, and then you don't have room to build and play! How do you think we can solve that problem?*
- *Who can show us a nice way to ask a friend to share the blocks?*

If children complain about running out of building materials in the middle of their play, try to borrow more. Also, if they complain of people walking into their structures and knocking them down, try rearranging the furniture so the building centers are not in high-traffic areas.

Step 2: Ongoing Open Explorations and Reflections

By continuing to explore building materials, children will develop important ideas and raise interesting questions about balance, stability, and characteristics of materials, while building the foundation they need for future, more focused explorations.

CORE EXPERIENCES

- ☐ Explore a variety of building materials.
- ☐ Share building experiences.

PREPARATION

- ☐ Display at eye level drawings you and children make of block structures.
- ☐ Review "Observation and Assessment" (p. 77) for strategies and tools to help capture children's level of engagement and their science understandings.

SCHEDULE

- ☐ 5–10 minutes for a meeting before each choice time
- ☐ 45–60 minutes for choice time every day until children have had repeated experiences exploring each building material
- ☐ 5–10 minutes every few days for a walkabout
- ☐ 5–10 minutes for discussion with the whole group

MATERIALS

Block area:

- ☐ Unit blocks

ISSUE: *My children love to build just to knock the blocks down!*

RESPONSE: There are a number of ways to move children through this stage. First, you might provide them with foam blocks to knock down outdoors. Second, when you begin taking photos or creating drawings of children's completed towers, they will be more inclined to create standing towers that can be captured on film or paper. Third, try establishing a rule that all structures need to be taken apart from the top down. Demonstrate this technique during a meeting with the whole group.

Add:

☐ Cardboard blocks

☐ Toy animals and dollhouse people

Building centers:

☐ Kapla or Dr. Drew blocks

☐ Foam blocks

Add:

☐ Colorful tabletop blocks or mini unit blocks

☐ Straws and connectors or small waffle blocks

☐ Cuisenaire rods, cube blocks, or large dominoes

☐ Small toy animals and dollhouse people

☐ Camera, if possible

☐ Copies of the observation record form (p. 93)

FAMILY CONNECTION

Send home notes suggesting families sign up to borrow bags of tabletop building materials over the weekend. Encourage family members to collect empty boxes and milk cartons, aluminum fish cans, or paper towel rolls for children to build with at home. (See "Families Building Structures" on p. 84, which suggests building materials and experiences families can share with children.)

TEACHING PLAN

ENGAGE

Before choice time, encourage and extend ongoing block play in a five- to ten-minute meeting with the whole group.

Encourage children to build.

Allow a few minutes during a meeting with the whole group, to encourage children's block play for the upcoming choice time.

Share a photo, drawing, or observation from a previous block play to engage and motivate builders. For example, you might say:

- *Remember the firehouse Megan and Sam built yesterday? It had room inside for two fire trucks. What do you think you'll build today?*

- *Caterina, I took this photograph of the house you built for the toy cats. Tell us about it. Who might build a house today?*

TEACHER NOTE: I can't believe the effect my enthusiasm for children's building has on their interest in choosing the block area or the building centers each day! Today I mentioned how much I enjoyed watching Alice and Christopher build and play with their troll bridge yesterday, and then more than half the class chose to use the building areas during choice time!

TEACHER NOTE: Ursile and Tony used the photos I took of the rocket they built yesterday to rebuild it today. They called the photos their "maps."

Introduce new building materials and new props.

In a whole group meeting before choice time, introduce the group to a new kind of building material, for example, some new blocks. Bring a few of these new blocks to the meeting and initiate a conversation with the children about them. You might ask:

- *What do you think you might build with these?*
- *How are these blocks or materials like some of the others you use?*
- *What do you think these blocks or materials will be good for building?*

Introduce the props in a way that encourages more block play. Ask children what they might build to house their toy animals, people, or vehicles. For example, you might ask:

- *These horses need a home that will keep them dry when it rains! What could we build for them?*
- *I've noticed that some of you like to read our books about castles. These people might like to live in one! Which kinds of blocks might you use to build a castle?*

EXPLORE

Acknowledge and support children's continued exploration.

Observe children's block play.

As children build, observe and document their play. You might do the following:

Children's Names	Seen and Heard
Cedrick	• building the John Hancock bldg! • likes the rug—"It's quiet when it falls." • Tries to stabilize the wall
Ahmed	• makes a "barn for my horse" • uses unit blocks flat as floor—rectangles up as walls

- Take photographs or make sketches of the structures children build.
- Write down the words children use to describe their structures.

TEACHER NOTE: When I introduced the Kapla blocks to the group, I put a couple in a paper bag ahead of time, and I shook the bag and asked the children to guess what kind of blocks were inside. They were quick to guess that the blocks weren't foam or plastic, or heavy! When I probed them to tell me why they eliminated foam blocks, they said it was because of the sound the shaking blocks made as they hit one another.

After I introduced the Kapla blocks to the group, Tara shared her idea about using them to build fences for our plastic animals.

- Use the observation record forms to note the kinds of structures children are constructing and the ways they position the materials. Are they building flat on the rug or table? Are they stacking the materials up? Are they making bridges? Are they building enclosures that are solid, or do the enclosures have space inside?

You will need this information to help you conduct science talks and decide when to begin a focused exploration of towers or enclosures.

Acknowledge children's block play.

When children are busy building, acknowledge them with a smile and observe their play. Model drawing structures by sitting with a clipboard and sketching the structures children build.

- If children show interest in your drawing, offer them paper and markers to make their own drawings.

- Talk with them about their drawings. Ask them to tell you about what they drew and to show you the parts of their structures that correspond to their drawings.

- If children are open to conversing as they build, or if they're taking a break, you might comment on the child's building strategy by saying something like: "I noticed that you put the roof block on very gently."

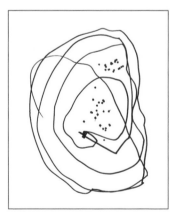

- Have the child describe a structure's design feature. For example, you could say: "There are so many windows in your firehouse!"

- Connect children's current building work to structures they've built in the past. For example, you can compare the size of a child's structure to one she built earlier in the week.

- Help children notice each other's block play. Comment on similarities and differences in children's structures and building strategies. You might comment on the way one child stacks blocks on their sides and another child stacks blocks on their ends. Or, you might comment on the different ways children make doorways.

TEACHER NOTE: I keep a class list on the back of each daily plan. I use it to take notes about the children's structures; for example, the nature of their play, how they're using the blocks, if they're being purposeful. I'm going to use these notes to help me decide when to move a group to a focused exploration.

TEACHER NOTE: Particularly in the beginning when I was encouraging children to draw their structures, I would draw what they were doing. Sometimes children would draw someone else's structure or sometimes that child would sit with me and draw their own too. That's when I would begin a conversation. For example, I'd say, "How did you get those to stay up so well?" It made them think about their building and allowed them an opportunity to explain things.

Christine was putting a foam cylinder across the top of two other ones standing up. It kept rolling off. Then she got it to balance and she drew this picture.

I asked her to show me the part in her drawing that was her tent. She traced her finger on the round part of her drawing and said, "It kept rolling off." I responded, "Hmm, I wonder what would happen if you built your tent using different blocks."

Encourage reluctant builders.

Children need a variety of opportunities to explore in each of the building centers. Use strategies such as these to encourage all children to participate in open exploration:

- Invite children to build with you.

- Partner an active builder with a reluctant one.

- Assign children to certain building centers during one or two choice times a week.

- Declare an "all girls" day in the block area.

- Put a chair in the building areas so children can choose to observe the building play.

TEACHER NOTE: Tyrone wasn't interested in building with blocks until I put the steering wheel into the block area.

TEACHER NOTE: I found a great way to get some of my non-builders into the building areas: first, I took photos of each child and each teacher in the class and taped them to separate blocks. My very social children were especially attracted to the photo-blocks and are building a castle for us all to live in!

Reflect

Conduct regular walkabouts and weekly science talks, allowing five to ten minutes for each.

Conduct a walkabout.

Help children notice, share, and reflect on one another's building experiences by organizing a walkabout every few days.

- At the end of choice time and before cleanup, gather your whole group and tell them that they are going on a walkabout to see some of the structures their friends built during choice time.

- Gather around the block area and invite children whose structures are standing there to tell the group about their structures.

- Move your group to each of the building centers and invite the builders to talk about what they have been building and playing.

Use what you know about their play to ask follow-up questions that focus on their building strategies and designs. For example, you might say the following:

- *I noticed that your roof fell in a few times. How did you get it to stay up this time?*

- *Can you show us how you made this long block balance in the middle of your rocket?*

- *What shape is your dog's house? How many blocks did you use to build it?*

Build children's structure vocabulary by comparing their building strategies and designs. For example, you might say the following:

- *I notice that the blocks at the bottom of Miguel's house are in the shape of a square, and so are the blocks at the bottom of the hospital Rita and Drew built.*

- *The dog house Olivia built has an arched doorway, and the firehouse Jean built does too!*

Conduct a science talk.

Help children share their building experiences and some of the ways they've been solving their building problems by organizing a science talk once a week. To focus children on a particular event, use a photo, a drawing, your notes, or a standing structure. You might say the following:

- *Yesterday I was watching Lilly build a house. She put one of these rectangle blocks on top of this one, but it fell off. She didn't put it back on; she chose a different one to put on top of the wall. Lilly, can you show us what you did? What happened when you put the square block on instead of the bigger, rectangular one?*

Issue: *How do I do a walkabout with my whole group? Our room is crowded and my children are active.*

Response: Begin slowly. During the first few walkabouts, you might visit just one building area. One teacher called the walkabouts "Museum Walks," which gave the children an idea of the kind of behavior she expected as they walked around the classroom and stood near fragile block structures.

Teacher note: My kids would love to keep their structures standing, but we just can't because we need room for the cots at rest time. However, since I've posted my drawings of their structures at eye level and right in the building areas, they rebuild their structures from one day to the next, adding and redesigning as they go.

Teacher note: There are so many opportunities to connect math to our block play. This is how Emily and Julia described their building to the rest of us during the walkabout: "We put two triangles together and a circle and a rectangle on top. There were two rectangles and a circle for the door."

Issue: *My children cannot sit and discuss things in a large group.*

Response: It definitely takes practice! Start with very short science talks. For example, you might describe a house you noticed children working on during the morning's choice time, and then you can direct children to see its specific features by sharing a sketch you made of it.

- *I was watching Madison build a cave for the polar bear yesterday. I noticed that the cave's walls fell in twice, but then Madison figured out a way to make the walls curve in and come together at the top. Madison, would you please show your friends how you did that? What did you notice Madison doing to keep the walls from falling in?*

Bring an enlarged photo or drawing of a child's structure to a whole group meeting before choice time. Invite the builder or builders to tell the group about their structure and block play. You might say or ask questions like these:

- *Tell us about your building.*

- *Which parts of it wiggled or fell down? How did you keep it up?*

- *What might you build today?*

Transition from Open Exploration to Focused Exploration

As children build with different kinds of materials during open exploration, they begin to notice how blocks of different shapes and sizes and made from different materials are good for different kinds of building. Through their actions and words they begin to ask questions about stability and balance, and notice characteristics of materials. For example, during open exploration a child may build up to see how high she can go before her structure wobbles or falls. Or a child may work to enclose toys inside a roofed structure so they're safe from imaginary rain.

During a focused exploration, children engage in an investigation that focuses on a question that is central to their particular interest. They make new observations and record and represent their experiences. These experiences can also lead to the formulation of new understandings or theories based on the evidence they have gathered.

When children begin to reflect on their actions and look for patterns and relationships in building structures, they often develop new questions. Samples of more focused questions include the following: How I can make a tall building that doesn't fall down? How I can build a house that's big enough for all my dogs and with a roof that will keep them dry but does not fall in on their heads?

If most of your children have been engaged in building with various materials over the past few weeks, many of them may have developed an interest in a particular structural challenge. Children who have had previous experiences playing with blocks may be ready for a focused

EXAMPLE: The photo (left) shows part of a science talk facilitated by one teacher. This excerpt begins after the builders told the group about the little tent they built on the platform.

Teacher: *I see that you used three Kapla blocks to build your tent. Can you show us how you built it using the Kapla blocks here?*

To the group: *What do you notice Kahlid doing to keep the tent from falling?*

Child 1: *Holding it until it doesn't fall.*

Teacher: *Kahlid, how do you know when to let go?*

Kahlid: *When these bottom parts aren't slipping.*

Child 1: *Look! It's the cracks in the platform that keep the tent from slipping!*

Encourage children to describe their structures in terms of mathematical attributes including shape, number, size, pattern, and order.

exploration before others. Or older children may be ready for a fo-cused exploration before some younger ones. There are some signs to look for to determine which children might like to pursue a more fo-cused question or exploration. These signs include the following:

- Spending a full choice time building

- Becoming deliberate in how they build their structures

- Choosing to build regularly

Focused exploration includes two different studies. The towers study appeals to children who are interested in building up, focusing their exploration on using designs and materials to affect their tall struc-ture's stability.

The enclosures study appeals to children who are interested in building structures with interior spaces, supports, and roofs. This study focuses children on the effects different kinds of building materials and designs have on construction of roofs, walls, doors, and windows.

You may notice that some children will remain engaged in open exploration and might want to continue to explore broadly, which is fine. They can continue with open exploration while others shift to focused exploration. Participating in the group discussions, observing, and listening to the children who are reflecting on their strategies for building tall towers or large enclosures will help those still in open exploration become interested in more focused building.

focused exploration: towers

Children have been playing with different kinds of building materials, experiencing how the stability of their structures is affected by the ways they put materials together and by the materials they use. Some of the children have become interested in stacking blocks; others build tall structures such as rockets and lookout towers as part of their block play. The focused exploration of towers is likely to appeal to these children, but all your children can and should be invited to participate.

When children build up, the forces of gravity, compression, and tension affect their structure's stability in dramatic ways. By working with different materials in various ways, children can experience and control the degree to which towers wobble and fall over. But children don't always have opportunities to think about how their choice of building materials and designs affect their structure's stability. So the focused exploration offers them opportunities to revisit, represent, and discuss their work. They are encouraged to reflect on evidence to support their developing theories about how building materials and designs affect a structure's stability.

Step 1: Introduce the Towers Exploration

This initial step helps you set the tone for an exciting and manageable exploration of building tall. It guides your thoughtful introduction of the focus on tower building, rules, and routines, and it introduces you to some of the strategies and roles you will be using to help children reflect on their work.

CORE EXPERIENCES

☐ Build tall towers.

☐ Represent towers.

☐ Reflect on the effects of designs and materials on the stability of tall towers.

PREPARATION

☐ Hang posters of skyscrapers and other tall structures around the classroom.

☐ Display books about tall buildings in the building centers and the block area.

SCHEDULE

☐ 5–10 minutes for a meeting before each choice time

☐ 45–60 minutes for choice times

☐ 5–10 minutes for a walkabout with the whole group

☐ 5–10 minutes for a science talk with the whole group

MATERIALS

☐ 4 or more child-size hard hats

☐ Camera, if possible

☐ Copies of the observation record form (p. 93)

FAMILY CONNECTION

Send a note home to families that introduces the topic of tall structures. Suggest that families borrow books about skyscrapers from their local library to look at with their children.

TEACHING PLAN

ENGAGE

Introduce the towers exploration with the whole group for five to ten minutes.

Share experiences.

Gather children together in a circle and invite them to share experiences they've had building up. Ask questions like these to help engage children in the discussion:

- *What have you built that's tall?*
- *What kinds of blocks did you use?*
- *How did you build it?*
- *How tall did it get?*

Show children photographs of some of the tall structures they have constructed, or gather them in a circle around one of the taller structures left standing in the classroom. Use questions or comments like these to guide discussion:

- *Tell me about this building.*
- *What do you think makes it strong?*
- *How did you keep it from falling down?*

Introduce a building challenge.

Tell the children that some of them might want to become expert tower builders by trying to build the tallest structures they can using one kind of block. Tell them that each of the building centers will be open for the next few weeks for tower building. Ask questions such as the following:

- *Which blocks do you think will be best for making tall towers? Why?*
- *Which towers do you think will get the tallest? Why?*

Discuss safe ways of building tall.

Have children use hard hats and a chair for protection when building up over their heads. When introducing the hats and chair, you might say the following:

- *Your towers could get taller than you! If your building gets as tall as your chin, you need to put on a hard hat. That way, if the tower falls down and the blocks hit your head, they won't hurt you.*
- *If you build a really tall tower and you can't reach the top to add more blocks, you can stand on this chair. This is a safe way of moving and standing on the chair. (Demonstrate how children should get on and off the chair.)*

EXPLORE

Support and encourage children to build "up" during this first week of the towers exploration.

Observe and acknowledge children's tower building.

Look for children's understanding of balance and stability. This is an important aspect of building towers. Use the observation record form (p. 93) to take notes as you observe in the building centers and the block area. Look for factors like these:

- The care with which children add blocks to their towers
- If they choose blocks that are likely to balance
- If they restructure parts of their structures to make them more stable

This example is from a teacher's conversation with her group as she introduced the towers focused exploration.

Teacher: *Tell us about your structure.*

Child 1: *It's the lighthouse!*

Child 2: *Here's the place where the guy lives, and here's the light at the top.*

Teacher: *How did you get it so tall?*

Child 2: *Well, this round one is where it kept falling.*

Teacher: *But then you got it to stay up. How did you do that?*

Child 1: *We didn't use any more round ones!*

Teacher: *Has anyone else made something tall that they can tell us about?*

ISSUE: *This sounds like a competition.*

RESPONSE: It's helpful to keep the focus on which blocks and designs make the tallest towers, rather than on *who* built the tallest tower.

TEACHER NOTE: At first I didn't really like the idea of kids standing on chairs. It didn't feel safe. But we talked about the rules and kids really got it. We put a sticker on the "Standing On" chair, and kids only use it when they need to build up.

Children's Names	Seen and Heard
Ronnie	• begins by putting row on table (call yellow!)—tabletop blocks. • builds up—trouble aligning blocks in tower
miguel	• constructs careful foundation with hollow blocks • symmetrical unit block tower about 2 feet high

When children are busy building towers, acknowledge their work with a smile and a descriptive comment about their structure. You might try comments like these:

- *I see a pattern in your tower. First you used two rectangles, then you used a cylinder, and then you added two more rectangles and another cylinder.*

- *This reminds me of the Eiffel Tower. It's wide at the bottom and becomes narrow at the top.*

Make sketches or take photographs of children building tall. You will use these notes and sketches to facilitate a science talk in a few days.

Encourage children who haven't shown interest in the tower challenge to build up.

As you visit the building areas, engage children in brief conversations. Ask them about their structures and then, in the context of their play, encourage them to build up. For example, you might say and ask the following:

- *Tell me about the house you're building. Can you add a chimney to it?*

- *Tell me about the fire station you're building. Can you build a lookout tower for the firefighters so they can look for smoke?*

- *Let's look at this book about castles. You can see what turrets look like and then add one to your castle.*

As children build up, you can help them use math to measure and describe structures. In addition to counting the number of blocks in a structure, children can use their bodies, string, Unifix cubes, and meter sticks to measure heights. They can also discuss patterns in their structures and the shapes of individual blocks and of entire buildings.

ISSUE: *I have children who are really interested in making homes for their animals or other things. I don't want to interfere with their focus.*

RESPONSE: By all means, support children as they follow their own ideas. Only some children may take up the challenge of building up at this time; others may do so later. Look for ways to talk about building up as children remain focused on their ideas.

REFLECT

Lead a walkabout and a science talk for five to ten minutes each at least once during the week.

Conduct a large group walkabout.

Before cleanup, gather the whole group together and take them on a walkabout to look at their friends' tall structures. As you visit each of the building centers and the block area, engage the builders with questions such as the following:

- *What kind of tall building is this? Have you ever seen or been in one like it?*

- *What did you do to keep it from falling?*

- *What happened to your block tower when you added that last block?*

- *What would happen if we took this block out of the tower?*

Conduct a large group science talk.

At the end of the week, gather your group together in a circle. Share drawings or photos of some of the towers children built during the week. Help them notice and describe different designs by asking questions such as the following:

- *Tell us about your structure. Do you think this is as tall as the tower could go before falling down? Why do you say that?*

- *I see that you placed the blocks on their flat side. What do you think might have happened if you'd used the thinner side of each block?*

- *Can you tell us about the pattern in your tower? How do you think the pattern helped to make the tower tall?*

- *This is the tower you built after your first one fell over. How did you build this one so it would stay up?*

TEACHER NOTE: I've always respected children's play and hesitate to interrupt it. But I am also convinced that it is important for them to have building experiences that allow them to collect data to develop their understandings of forces and materials and the influences both have on the stability of structures. So now I look for opportunities to enter children's play with suggestions for ways children who are building low or flat structures can add taller elements.

EXAMPLE: I showed Victor a picture of a submarine with its periscopes up, and he used it to add height to his "boat," which he now calls his "submarine."

TEACHER NOTE: The class and I discussed strategies for tower building. Sasha suggested, "The bottom has a lot of weight and is holding it up." Ian said, "The ones on the bottom are holding it up. I put extra at the bottom so it won't fall down—so it will hold more."

Step 2: Ongoing Towers Explorations

The more opportunities children have to build towers, represent them, and reflect on their experiences, the better. These experiences provide children with the evidence they need to refine their ideas about balance and stability, and the characteristics of materials.

CORE EXPERIENCES

☐ Build, measure, and represent towers.

☐ Look at books about towers.

☐ Discuss children's developing ideas about balance and stability, and characteristics of materials.

PREPARATION

☐ Ask colleagues and families to recommend an architect, builder, or structural engineer to visit the classroom. Arrange for the guest to meet with your whole group sometime in the next couple of weeks. See the extensions section (p. 69) for more information on planning for guest experts.

☐ If your school is near other buildings, walk around the block and note which ones have interesting tall features such as chimneys, steeples, and clock towers. Set a date in the next couple of weeks to take your children for a walk to look at tall structures. Arrange for adult volunteers to walk with your group. See the extensions section (p. 67) for information on planning a focused structures field trip or walk.

☐ Identify a table near the building centers to use as a center for making three-dimensional models of tall structures built in the block area and building centers.

SCHEDULE

☐ 5 minutes for a meeting before each choice time

☐ 45–60 minutes for choice time, four or five days a week, until all interested children have had multiple opportunities to build up

☐ 5–10 minutes for a walkabout, once a week

☐ 5–10 minutes for a science talk, once a week

MATERIALS

Block area:

☐ Unit blocks

☐ Cardboard blocks

☐ Toy animals and dollhouse people

☐ 4 or more child-size hard hats

☐ 4 or more clipboards with paper and markers

Continue the towers exploration until all interested children have had repeated opportunities to participate.

Add:

☐ Books with photos or drawings of tall buildings

☐ Pieces of chart paper cut in thirds or other long paper for representational drawing

Building centers:

☐ Kapla or Dr. Drew blocks

☐ Foam blocks

☐ Colorful tabletop blocks or mini unit blocks

☐ Cuisenaire rods, cube blocks, or large dominoes

☐ Small toy animals and dollhouse people

☐ 2 or more clipboards, paper, and markers at each building center

Add:

☐ Straws and connectors or small waffle blocks

☐ Books with photos or drawings of tall buildings

Add a model-building table and include the following:

☐ Pieces of corrugated cardboard for bases to build on

☐ Cardboard tubes

☐ Empty boxes

☐ Pieces of foam

☐ Styrofoam

☐ Popsicle sticks

☐ Glue

☐ Masking tape

☐ Clay

☐ Coffee stirrers

☐ Paint

☐ Camera, if possible

☐ Copies of the observation record form (p. 93)

☐ Chart: "What Makes a Tower Tall and Stable?"

FAMILY CONNECTION

Suggest families build towers at home. If they have blocks at home, of course these can be used, but other materials such as boxes, cans, egg cartons, and packing foam can all be used for building as well. Invite them to send a sketch of a tower they built together to school along with their child. Some families may want to include a description of how they got their tower to stay standing. Create a bulletin board of the sketches and children's descriptions of these at-home building experiences.

TEACHING PLAN

ENGAGE

Keep the momentum going. At this point in the exploration, sharing documentation of children's work, helping them to expand on their previous buildings, and providing new ways of building and representing their buildings will help children stay engaged in the study of building tall.

Encourage building.

Allow a few minutes in a meeting with the whole group to encourage children to build up during the upcoming choice time. Share a photo, drawing, or observation from a previous block play to engage and motivate builders. For example, you might say the following:

- *Remember the tall cardboard block tower Jillian and Sam built yesterday? Jillian, how might you two make it taller today?*
- *Yesterday Allison used this piece of string to measure her Kapla block tower. If you want her to show you how, I'm sure she'd be happy to during choice time.*

Look at pictures of tall buildings.

Use picture books and posters of tall buildings to inspire your builders. As a whole group or with small groups, study the pictures together. To initiate conversation, ask questions such as the following:

- *Have you ever seen a building like this? Tell us about it.*
- *How would you build a tower like the one in the picture?*

Conduct a walkabout.

Use local buildings to inspire your builders. Lead small and large group walkabouts around the block to look at tall buildings and towerlike parts of buildings. Ask questions such as the following:

- *What's special about this building?*
- *How do you think it is different from the one next to it?*

Help children notice features of buildings that are towerlike, for example, chimneys, steeples, and clock towers. Ask them questions such as the following:

- *What do you think keeps the chimney from falling off the roof?*
- *How do you think the builders made the clock tower so it won't fall over?*

ISSUE: *I have children who play at one of the block centers for a whole week, and then they lose interest and don't go back.*

RESPONSE: Children typically "take a break" from building. Entice them back with props that appeal to one of their interests. For example, perhaps you could find them small dolls or action figures that could become Rapunzel or knights for a castle.

TEACHER NOTE: I have a group of children who love the Madeline books, so they recognized the Eiffel Tower as soon as I taped up the poster. They like to build the tower and then play Madeline with the dollhouse people.

TEACHER NOTE: When I walked around the block with my group, we stopped at the park behind our school. We've been talking about patterns, and Alicia said she saw one in the wall.

Invite a guest expert to talk with the group.

Introduce children to a dramatic role they can play while building by inviting a guest expert such as an architect, builder, or mason into the classroom. Ask visitors to talk about what they do and to share designs, tools, books, and stories related to their work. Allow children the opportunity to ask questions, and invite them to share their structures or drawings with visitors. Add props such as an architect's drawing tools to the building centers so children can incorporate dramatic play into the towers exploration.

EXAMPLE: Samuel shared his tower and his drawing with our visiting carpenter.

See the extension activities (pp. 69–70) for more information on inviting a guest expert into the classroom to enhance the exploration.

EXAMPLE: Julia calls herself an architect whenever she uses the drafting tools.

EXPLORE

Support and encourage children as they continue to build up.

Observe and acknowledge children's building.

Children's Names	Seen and Heard
Sharika	• builds flat with foam • says "You can't build good with these."
Alex	• says "Look! You can. Ella and me can." • makes sure blocks are straight
Ella	• works with Alex to build tall tower (foam)

Continue to observe children's tower building, noticing their understanding of balance and stability, and characteristics of materials. Use the observation record form (p. 93) to note building characteristics like these:

- When and why they build symmetrically
- If or how they redesign toppled towers to be more stable
- If or how they take more care placing blocks as they rebuild toppled towers
- If or how their designs change when they switch building materials

Sketch or photograph children's towers whenever possible.

- Acknowledge persistent builders by saying something like this: "You've been working on that structure for a long time. You don't give up easily!"
- Acknowledge collaboration by saying something like this: "It's great to see the way you two take turns putting blocks on your tower."

Talk with interested children.

Some children will want to tell you about their towers. Use these opportunities to listen to their descriptions and help them reflect on their building strategies by asking questions such as the following:

- *Tell me about this tower.*
- *Tell me about the things you do to keep it from getting too wobbly.*
- *Why did you decide to use that block in your tower?*

Encourage reluctant builders.

Use strategies like these to encourage all children to participate in the towers exploration.

- Invite children to build with you.
- Partner an active builder with a reluctant one.
- Assign children to certain building centers during one or two choice times a week.

Child 1: *Look, Teacher! They jump off!*

Teacher: *Wow! That's a tall tower for them to jump off of. How did you get the tower to stay up?*

Child 2: *We don't let go till it's stopped wiggling.*

Teacher: *You two girls built two towers, one with Kapla blocks and one with waffle blocks. What did you find out?*

Child 1: *We figured out that these Kapla blocks aren't so strong. Those (waffle blocks) are stronger.*

Child 2: *Yeah, because those connect together, but these ones pile up on each other, and every time someone puts their shoulder on it, they go "whoosh." Even if you just gently touch. "Whoosh."*

The example above illustrates how one teacher helped children reflect on what they were learning about different building materials.

TEACHER NOTE: I had a group of children that weren't participating in the towers exploration at all until I sat with them and looked through a book about skyscrapers. The images really gave the kids a starting point. Now we're looking at the parts of their block structures that are like the ones in the books.

TEACHER NOTE: My girls were drawn into the block area as soon as I made the people blocks.

- Declare an "all girls" day in the block area.

- Put a chair in the building areas so children can choose to observe the building play.

- Tape photographs of children in your class on blocks.

- Display postcards, picture books, and posters of skyscrapers in the different building areas.

Some children like to build when they know they can put a Please Save sign on their structure and keep it up for the day, or longer.

Encourage children to make representational drawings of their tall structures.

Have long paper, markers, and drafting tools available in or next to the building centers. Encourage children to draw their structures during choice time or before cleanup, and remind them to look at their structures as they draw. If there are reluctant drawers, use encouraging comments like these:

Three- and four-year-olds made these representational drawings.

- *What shape is your tower? Now try to draw that shape on your paper.*

- *Juan started by drawing the bottom block, and then the one on top of it, all the way until they get to the top. You could do that.*

- *How many blocks are in your tower? Now you can draw a six-block tower on your paper.*

Model the process by continuing to draw children's structures. When children are ready to share their representational drawings with you, you might make comments like this one:

- *Tell me about your drawing. What part(s) of your building did you show?*

Use follow-up questions to help children make connections between the details of their structure and those in their drawings. You might make comments like these:

- *Your tower is tall. Show me the lines on your paper that show your tall tower.*

- *You called the top block on your skyscraper "the crown." Can you show me where the crown is in your drawing?*

- *What shapes did you use in your drawing? Where are those shapes in your tower?*

- *The blocks in your drawing are tipping to the side. Is that what happened when you built your tower? How did you keep the blocks from tipping over?*

TEACHER NOTE: I brought a white-board and markers over to the block area because Abigail was having a hard time imagining what her tower would look like if it were built with blocks placed vertically instead of horizontally, as she had done. Not only did it help her to see a drawing of a tower built with verticals, but Adam came up to the drawing and pointed to one of the blocks near the top of the drawing, declaring that he didn't think it would balance on top of the one under it. So he and Abigail proceeded to use the drawing to build a tower and, lo and behold, Adam was right! Tomorrow I'm going to invite him to tell the group about the event. We can ask Adam how he knew that the vertical wouldn't balance.

Opportunities for making math connections abound as children create and talk about their representational drawings. You might ask questions such as: What shapes do you see? How many blocks did you draw? How tall did it get? What patterns do you see?

Encourage children to make representational models of their tall structures.

Have collage materials, glue, tape, and scissors available at a table near the building centers.

During choice time, invite small groups of tower builders to the table and introduce the concept of making a model. Together, look at the collage materials and think about which ones might work well to model the kinds of blocks the builders have been using. It sometimes takes time for children to construct a model of their structures. They might finish work all in one day, or they might work for a few minutes each day during a week.

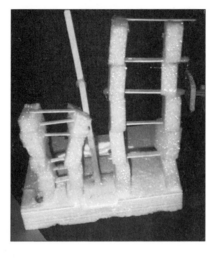

Encourage children to look at the actual block structure while they construct their model. If this isn't possible, draw or take a photograph of the original block structure and make it available during the model-making process. When children are ready to share the models, just as you do when they share their drawings, encourage conversation with a statement such as this: "Tell me how you made this." Use follow-up questions to help children make connections between their block structures and their models. You might say and ask the following:

- *I notice that you put the big unit blocks at the bottom of your lookout tower, and you've glued the biggest boxes down to make the bottom of your model.*

- *Which block in your tower was the hardest to balance? Where is that piece in your model? Was it hard to balance too? I wonder why.*

EXAMPLE: As Patrick used foam pieces to make a model of his cylinder unit block tower, he noticed that the foam tower was much less stable than the one made of wooden blocks.

Three- and four-year-olds made these models of unit block structures.

TEACHER NOTE: Sam's model of his tower wouldn't stand because it was made out of cardboard and his original structure had been built with unit blocks, which are much heavier. As he solved the problem of how to keep his model standing (he taped rocks on the bottom supports), we talked about why he thought he needed so much weight to keep it steady.

Encourage children to measure their towers.

To encourage children to measure their towers' heights, you might try the following:

- Count the number of blocks in a child's tower and invite children to count along with you.

- Stand next to a child's structure and measure its height against you. Invite children to do the same.

- Provide measuring tapes, string, or Unifix cubes as measuring tools.

Record the measurement data by inviting children to help you do some of the following:

- Write the number of blocks in a child's tower on a card and place the card next to the tower. Later, tape the card next to the child's representational drawing or a photo of the tower.

- Cut string to the height of a child's tower and tape it to the wall. Tape the child's representational drawing or a photograph of the tower next to the string.

- Take photographs of children measuring their towers against themselves or against a friend or adult. Use the photographs to make a documentation panel focused on the strategies children use to build taller towers.

EXAMPLE: Christine used her body to measure the height of her tower.

ISSUE: *I worry that my children's preoccupation with whose tower is the tallest is taking away from the learning experience.*

RESPONSE: Focus on the positive attributes of each child's structure. For example, you might say: "This building Joe built is very strong. Alex, yours is quite tall but I wonder if you could use some of Joe's ideas to make it stronger, and he can use some of your ideas to make his taller."

Encourage children to build with a combination of materials.

Remind children that they might want to use building materials from different areas of the classroom and combine them in their structures. As you visit the building centers, engage children in conversations about what they notice when they combine materials to build tall structures. For example, you might ask questions like these:

- *What happened when you put the unit block on the foam?*

- *I noticed you put the heavier blocks on the bottom. How come?*

- *What do you think would happen if . . . ?*

- *Why did you put the squishier blocks on the bottom?*

- *Why did you use cardboard blocks instead of unit blocks?*

Document children's experiences.

Use your photographs and children's work to create a documentation panel that shows how children are developing strategies for building tall structures. Include a few sentences about how they made their discoveries. See "Guidelines for Creating Documentation Panels" (p. 92) for guidance. You will need this panel for future science talks.

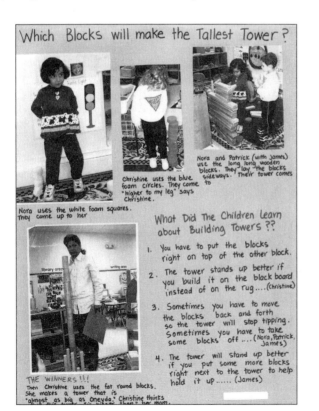

Which Blocks will make the Tallest Tower?

Nora uses the white foam squares. They come up to her

Christine uses the blue foam circles. They come to "higher to my leg" says Christine

Nora and Patrick (with James) use the long long wooden blocks. They lay the blocks sideways. Their tower comes to

What Did The Children Learn about Building Towers??

1. You have to put the blocks right on top of the other block.

2. The tower stands up better if you build it on the black board instead of on the rug....(Christine)

3. Sometimes you have to move the blocks back and forth so the tower will stop tipping. Sometimes you have to take some blocks off....(Nora, Patrick, James)

4. The tower will stand up better if you put some more blocks right next to the tower to help hold it up......(James)

THE WINNERS!!!
Then Christine uses the fat round blocks. She makes a tower that is "almost as big as Oneyda." Christine thinks

Teacher note: Brianna was eager to share her tall house with me.

> **Teacher:** *What happened to the piece of foam when you put these three unit blocks on top of it?*
>
> **Brianna:** *It bended!*
>
> **Teacher:** *What do you think would have happened if you'd used a unit block here instead of the foam?*
>
> **Brianna:** *It wouldn't be a soft place. But it would be straight!*

When builders use materials of a different shape, size, texture, and density in a single building, they confront the effect forces have on the combinations and present them with opportunities to deepen their understanding of materials and their characteristics.

Teacher note: The children have been talking about making their towers "the same on both sides." I'm collecting photos and their drawings to make a documentation panel to show the symmetry in their towers.

REFLECT

Facilitate a walkabout and a science talk each week, allowing five to ten minutes for each one.

Conduct weekly walkabouts to share and discuss children's tall buildings.

Once a week, or when there are particularly interesting structures to look at, gather your whole group together at the end of choice time for a walkabout. As builders share their tall structures, help them reflect on the strategies they used. You might ask questions like these:

- *How did you get your [tower, rocket, chimney, etc.] to stay up?*

- *Which part of your structure do you think is the strongest? Why do you think so?*

- *Which part do you think was the trickiest to build? Why do you think so?*

Conduct weekly science talks focused on balance and stability.

Once a week and for at least two weeks, gather your whole group together in a circle so children can share and analyze their developing ideas about building towers that are tall and stable. If children are interested, focus additional science talks on the strategies they use to build tall structures. If possible, meet in the block area, or bring some blocks to the meeting. Then focus the science talk by reading the question on the chart you prepared ahead of time: "What Makes a Tower Tall and Stable?" Encourage children to demonstrate their ideas with the blocks. Share a few photos of the children's towers that are tall but designed differently. Use follow-up questions such as these:

- *If you want to build a strong lookout tower, like for one of the airports you've been building, what are some good ways to start?*

- *What are some of the ways you kept the lookout tower from falling down? Rhonda says it works best to put lots of big blocks down first, and then start building up. What do you think, Dan?*

- *Mark, can you show us what you mean when you say you have to take your hand off the block after it's straight?*

TEACHER NOTE: When Matt shared the structure he made out of Dr. Drew blocks during today's walkabout, he told us that he "made the walls double thick to make it strong."

TEACHER NOTE: At the beginning of the towers exploration, I asked: "What makes a strong structure?" Their answers weren't very detailed and they weren't specific, but now I notice their answers are more specific: "You need to use the big blocks on the bottom, the smaller blocks on top, and if it starts to wiggle, you need to hold it with your hands and straighten it out." They are getting so much experience! I think that balance and stability is the biggest part of what they're learning.

We compared this tower to the earlier ones children built that were just stacks of cardboard blocks, one on top of the other. Philip insists that triangle-shaped towers are the strongest.

Conduct science talks focused on characteristics of materials.

Once a week and for two additional weeks, gather your whole group together in a circle so children can share and analyze their ideas about the pros and cons of building towers with different kinds of blocks. If interest is high, focus additional science talks on characteristics of materials. If possible, meet in the block area, or bring a few of each of the kinds of blocks children have been using to build up to the science talk. Also, share a few photos of towers children built with different kinds of blocks. Focus the science talk on characteristics of materials by referring back to the "What Makes a Tower Tall and Stable?" chart you used earlier. Use follow-up questions and comments like these:

- *Randy, here's a picture of your foam tower.*
  - *What was hard about using foam blocks to build up so tall?*
  - *What was good about using foam blocks?*
  - *What did you do to make the tower stand up? Can you show us?*

- *Alden and Mira built a lookout tower out of unit blocks.*
  - *What do you two like about building with unit blocks?*
  - *How did you get your lookout tower to be so tall and strong?*

Encourage children to find out more about which blocks make the best tall towers during upcoming choice times. Tell them that you can add their ideas to the chart during the week.

TEACHER NOTE: We gathered around the double skyscraper Ali built during choice time. Ali was so proud as he talked about how he built it. I asked why he decided to put the foam blocks at the top of the unit block tower and he said, "They'd get squished on the bottom."

And I asked, "Squished isn't good?"

Ali replied, "Well, it's tippy."

And then Lila had an "aha": "Oh! Like when I stand on my bed!"

SAMPLE CHART.

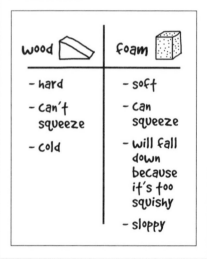

wood	foam
– hard	– soft
– can't squeeze	– can squeeze
– cold	– will fall down because it's too squishy
	– sloppy

ISSUE: *It seems arbitrary to focus on characteristics of materials during one conversation, and balance and stability during another science talk. They're so linked!*

RESPONSE: Yes, they are completely intertwined. The intension is not to separate the two as if they weren't related but to focus on one or the other so children can articulate and identify their theories about how each affects their attempts to build up.

focused exploration: enclosures

Children have been playing with different kinds of building materials, experiencing how their structures' stability is affected by the ways they put materials together and by what materials they use. Some children have become interested in building houses, forts, garages, or other kinds of enclosures as part of their block play. The enclosures focused exploration appeals to these children, but all your children can and should be exposed to the focused exploration of enclosures because, when children build structures that have walls and a roof, the forces of gravity, compression, and tension affect the stability of the walls and how large a roof-load they can bear. But children don't always have opportunities to notice how their choice of building materials and designs affect their structure's stability. So the focused explorations offer them opportunities to revisit, represent, and discuss their work, which encourages them to use evidence to support their developing theories about how building materials and designs affect their structure's stability.

Step One: Introduce the Enclosures Exploration

This initial step helps you set the tone for an exciting and manageable exploration of enclosures. It guides your thoughtful introduction of a focus on how a builder's choice of design and materials can affect the way their building's walls, corners, windows, and doors respond to a load-bearing roof. It also introduces you to some of the strategies and roles you will be using to help children reflect on their work.

CORE EXPERIENCES

□ Build and represent enclosures.

□ Reflect on how the stability of enclosures is affected by designs and materials.

PREPARATION

□ Hang posters of large enclosures such as stadiums, malls, airports, and factories around the classroom at children's eye level.

□ Display books with images of enclosures in the building centers and the block area. (See p. 82 in the resources section for suggestions.)

SCHEDULE

□ 5–10 minutes for a whole class meeting before each choice time

□ 45–60 minutes for choice time each day for a week

□ 5–10 minutes for a walkabout

□ 5–10 minutes for a whole group discussion

MATERIALS

Block area:

□ Unit blocks

□ Cardboard blocks

□ Toy animals and dollhouse people

Add:

□ 4 or more clipboards with paper and markers

□ Hollow or large waffle blocks

□ Roof materials—for example, different-size pieces of cardboard, unit block roof boards, or old bedsheets

Building centers:

□ Kapla or Dr. Drew blocks

□ Foam blocks

□ Colorful tabletop blocks or mini unit blocks

□ Straws and connectors or waffle blocks

□ Cuisenaire rods, cube blocks, or large dominoes

□ Small toy animals and dollhouse people

Add:

□ 2 or more clipboards at each building center

□ Roof materials—for example, pieces of fabric about 6 inches square or different-size pieces of cardboard

☐ Camera, if possible

☐ Copies of the observation record form (p. 93)

FAMILY CONNECTION

Send a note home to families that introduces the focus on enclosures. Suggest that families borrow books about building houses from their local library to look at with their children. Also, ask whether anyone has building expertise they would like to share.

TEACHING PLAN

ENGAGE

Introduce the enclosures exploration with the whole group for five to ten minutes.

Discuss children's experiences with building enclosures.

Gather children together in a circle. Point out that some of the structures they build have places inside for people, animals, cars, and other things. Invite children to share experiences they've had building these kinds of structures or enclosures by asking questions like these:

- *Have you ever built a house out of blocks?*
- *What did it look like?*
- *Who lived in it?*
- *How big was it?*

Show children photographs of enclosures they have constructed, or gather them in a circle around one of the enclosures left standing in the classroom. You might ask questions like these:

- *Tell me about this building. Who or what goes in it? Can you show us?*
- *Does it have different rooms? Does it have a door?*
- *How did you get the roof to stay on? How did you keep it from falling down?*

Introduce new materials for roofs and floors.

Tell children that they might want to build bigger, fancier houses (such as garages, hideouts, spaceships, and so on) using some new materials you've collected for the block centers. Share the materials you have collected for this purpose, and tell them that each of the building centers will be open for the next week or two for building structures with doors, walls, floors, and roofs. Ask questions like these:

- *What do you think you'll build today?*
- *Will it have different stories or different rooms?*
- *Who or what will go in it?*
- *Will it stay dry if it rains?*

TEACHER NOTE: Jacob said his leopard's house was in the jungle and he goes into it when he's tired. It keeps him safe and dry. I asked him how he got the roof to stay on. He said, "It goes from here to here," and he pointed to each of the sidewalls.

Review building guidelines.

Decide together where the new materials will be stored so children have easy access to them. Include children in creating new rules for using and caring for the materials. For example, ask for volunteers to show the group how they might carefully carry the larger pieces of cardboard.

EXPLORE

Support and encourage children to build enclosures during the beginning of the enclosures exploration.

Observe and acknowledge children as they build enclosures.

Observe children to see how or if they are integrating the new materials into their block play. Make sketches or take photographs of the ways children arrange blocks to hold up a roof, add a story, or make a door. When children are busy building various enclosures, acknowledge their work with a smile and a descriptive comment about their structure. For example, you might say something like this:

- *You've made a bed for each of the cats that live in the house.*

- *I'd love to live in a castle with so many rooms.*

Children's Names	Seen and Heard
Mia	• Kapla "tunnel"—roof supported by walls and interior row of double flat blocks • "These walls kept falling."
Alexander	• cardboard block "house" • door, no windows • each wall one block long

Have photographs and sketches from a previous building day available so children can use them as inspiration or as references. Use your notes and sketches to help children reflect on how they keep the walls, roofs, or additional stories of their enclosures from collapsing. You will need this information for the upcoming science talk and walkabout.

Class Meetings: Young Children Solving Problems Together by Emily Vance and Patricia Jimenez Weaver (Washington, D.C.: NAEYC, 2002) is a good resource for teachers who are interested in helping children come together to reflect on management issues.

Encourage builders who haven't yet shown interest in building enclosures.

As you visit the building centers, engage children in brief conversations. Ask them about their structures and then, in the context of their play, encourage them to add enclosures. For example, you might say something like this:

- *Tell me about the road you're making. Can you make some tunnels for the cars to go through?*

- *You've made a cozy bed for your dog. Can you make him a house too?*

- *Your tower reminds me of the lighthouse in this book. And look at the house the lighthouse keeper lives in! Can you make one?*

REFLECT

Facilitate a walkabout and a science talk during the week, allowing five to ten minutes for each.

Conduct a large group walkabout.

Once or twice during the week, just before cleanup, gather the whole group together for a walkabout to look at their friends' structures. As you visit each of the building centers and the block area, focus on the enclosures and engage the builders with questions such as the following:

- *What kind of building is this?*

- *Have you ever seen or been in one like it?*

- *How did you make the walls?*

- *How did you make the roof?*

- *What happened to the corners when you added the roof?*

- *What would happen if we took this block out and made a door?*

TEACHER NOTE: Gabi told me about her house: it has a big front porch, a front door, two side doors, and a balcony. She said it's the house she's going to live in when she grows up and that it has lots of places in it to go. When I asked to see those places, she realized her house was solid all the way through! That's when she added a bedroom for herself on the top floor, and it has four walls, and a roof, and when you look in the window, you can see a tiny bed.

TEACHER NOTE: After Sophia told the group about the railway station she built, I asked her what happened when she added the unit blocks across the roof. She said they first made the roof and walls wiggle, and then the wiggling stopped. I also asked her how she made it stronger and where she put the blocks.

Facilitate a science talk to help children share their developing ideas about how their building designs affect the parts of their enclosures—for example, the walls and corners, roofs, stories, doors, and windows.

Bring your group together in a circle and share drawings or photos of some of the enclosures children built during the week. Help children notice and describe the different ways they supported roofs, added stories, or created windows and doors by asking questions like these:

- *Tell us about your structure.*

- *How did you build the walls? What happened when you added the roof?*

- *What shapes do you think make the best roofs? Why do you say that?*

- *How did you build the window?*

TEACHER NOTE: I shared this photo with the whole group and used these questions to help them focus on span, support, and walls:

How did you build the roof?

What do you think would happen if you put the blocks across the other way, between the other two walls?

Why do you say that?

Step 2: Ongoing Enclosures Explorations

The more opportunities children have to build enclosures, represent them, and reflect on their experiences, the better. These experiences provide children with the evidence they need to refine their ideas about balance and stability, and the characteristics of materials.

CORE EXPERIENCES

☐ Build, describe, and represent enclosures.

☐ Look at books about enclosures.

☐ Discuss developing ideas about balance and stability, and characteristics of materials.

PREPARATION

☐ Ask colleagues and families to recommend an architect, builder, or structural engineer to visit the classroom. Arrange for the guest to meet with your whole group sometime within the next couple of weeks. See the extension activities section (p. 69) for more information on planning for guest experts.

☐ If your school is near other buildings, walk around the block and look for enclosures with exposed beams and pillars. Also, note any exposed fire escapes, scaffolding, balconies, or porches children can look at to see how roofs and floors are held up. Set a date in the next couple of weeks to take your children for a walk to look at tall structures. Arrange for adult volunteers to walk with your group. See the extension activities section (p. 67) for more information on planning a field trip or walk focused on enclosures.

SCHEDULE

- ☐ 5 minutes for a meeting before each choice time
- ☐ 45–60 minutes for choice time, four or five days a week, until all interested children have had multiple opportunities to build up
- ☐ 5–10 minutes for a walkabout each week
- ☐ 5–10 minutes for a science talk each week

MATERIALS

Block area:

- ☐ Unit blocks
- ☐ Cardboard blocks
- ☐ Hollow or large waffle blocks
- ☐ Toy animals and dollhouse people

Roof materials:

- ☐ Different-size pieces of cardboard
- ☐ Unit block roof boards
- ☐ Old bedsheets

Add:

- ☐ Books with photos or drawings of enclosures with various kinds of roofs

Building centers:

- ☐ Kapla or Dr. Drew blocks
- ☐ Foam blocks
- ☐ Colorful tabletop blocks or mini unit blocks
- ☐ Straws and connectors or waffle blocks
- ☐ Cuisenaire rods, cube blocks, or large dominoes
- ☐ Toy animals and dollhouse people
- ☐ 2 or more clipboards at each building center

Add:

- ☐ Books with photos or drawings of enclosures with various kinds of roofs

Continue the enclosures exploration until all interested children have had repeated opportunities to participate.

Add a model-building table with the following:

☐ Pieces of corrugated cardboard for bases to build on

☐ Cardboard tubes

☐ Empty boxes

☐ Pieces of foam

☐ Styrofoam

☐ Popsicle sticks

☐ Glue

☐ Masking tape

☐ Clay

☐ Paint

☐ Camera, if possible

☐ Copies of the observation record form (p. 93)

☐ Chart: "What We Know about Building Enclosures"

FAMILY CONNECTION

Send a note home asking families to collect paper towel rolls, empty food boxes, pieces of cardboard, and other scrounged materials to add to your model-making supplies. Invite family members to share with their children photos or illustrations of houses and buildings that are important to them. Suggest they sketch a picture of the house or building on paper and write a sentence or two about what makes it special to them. Have their child bring the picture to class to share, or suggest they visit the classroom to share the picture and its significance with the group.

TEACHING PLAN

ENGAGE

Keep the momentum going. At this point in the exploration, sharing documentation of children's work, helping them to expand on their previous buildings, and providing new ways of building and representing their buildings will help children stay engaged in the study of building enclosures.

Connect children's building experiences.

Allow a few minutes in a meeting with the whole group to encourage children to build enclosures during the upcoming choice time. Share a photo, drawing, or observation from a previous block play to engage and motivate builders. For example, you might say the following:

TEACHER NOTE: Children were ignoring the small unit blocks at the building center until I showed a photo of children building a hospital structure with the same blocks. Now children are working day after day on an elaborate hospital scene.

- *Remember the fire station Nina and Chris built yesterday? Here's the book they used to help them remember what a fire station looks like. I'll put it back in the building center by the windows for anyone else who wants to use it.*

- *I wasn't sure all of you got to see the circus tent Eli and Taylor built yesterday, so I sketched it on this paper. They used the cloth and blocks in the building center near the door. If you want to learn how to make circus tents, ask Eli and Taylor to show you.*

Introduce children to the idea of building structures to withstand wind.

Introduce children to the idea of building structures that can withstand outdoor elements such as the wind. Read a version of "The Three Little Pigs" aloud to a small group of children. Facilitate a short discussion about the ways the pigs' houses responded to the wolf's huffing and puffing. For example, you might ask the following questions:

- *Why do you think the wolf was able to blow down the straw house and the stick house, but not the brick one?*

- *What do you think would have happened if the brick house had been built without mortar and the pig tried to blow it down?*

- *Which of our classroom building materials do you think you would you use to make a house that could not be blown down?*

- *What if you did want the house to blow down?*

Close the meeting by asking children what kinds of blocks they think might make windproof enclosures, and then invite them to try their ideas during choice time.

Look at picture books of enclosures with children.

Use picture books of enclosures to inspire your builders, and as a whole group or with small groups, study the pictures together.
    To initiate conversation, use questions such as the following:

- *Have you ever seen a building like this? Tell us about it.*

- *How would you build one like the one in the picture? How would you keep the roof up?*

A child demonstrates blowing on a structure made of foam, Kapla, and unit blocks.

TEACHER NOTE: We read versions of "The Three Little Pigs" and talked about the different materials the pigs used to build their homes. I asked, "Which material do you think is the strongest?"

Child 1: *Bricks!*

Teacher: *Why?*

Child 2: *You can build with them. You can stick them together. You can put sticks together, but not straw.*

Child 3: *Because there's some kind of material in them that makes them strong. And if you try to fall them down, there's a material in the bricks that makes them stay up.*

Child 4: *There's some kind of sticky stuff that holds them together.*

Child 1: *Mortar.*

Child 4: *Sticks are lined up together. But if you don't have glue or nails, they slip.*

See the resources section on pp. 82–87 for more information on using books and Web sites to enhance the exploration.

Conduct a walkabout to look at local enclosures.

Use local buildings to inspire your builders. As a whole group or with small groups, walk around the block to look at structures that have exposed beams, supports, floors, or roofs. Fire escapes, garages, and balconies are good examples of these kinds of structures. Ask questions such as the following:

- *How is this roof like ones you've seen before?*

- *What do you think holds this roof up?*

Invite a guest expert to talk with the group.

- Introduce children to a dramatic role they can play while they build. Invite a professional architect, builder, engineer, or mason into the classroom, or invite an amateur carpenter or builder to come talk with the children.

- Ask the visitor to talk about what they do, and invite them to share designs, tools, books, and stories related to their work. Give children a chance to ask questions. Invite children to share their structures or drawings with the visitor.

- If possible, add props such as architectural drawing tools to the building centers so children can incorporate dramatic play into the towers exploration.

See the extension activities section on pp. 67–69 for more information on visiting local buildings to enhance the exploration.

TEACHER NOTE: After mia's aunt, an architect, visited the class and showed us how she draws plans for builders as part of her job, I set up a table and created an architect's office. Thalia has been there every day this week!

See the extension activities section on pp. 69–70 for more information on inviting a guest expert into the classroom to enhance the exploration.

EXPLORE

Support and encourage children as they continue to build enclosures.

Observe and acknowledge children's building.

Continue to observe children's building, noticing especially their understanding of compression and tension. Use the observation record form (p. 93) to document the following:

- *Are they building walls that are strong enough to hold up a roof?*
- *Are they building corners that resist being pushed apart when the roof goes on?*
- *Are they adding supports to their buildings before the roof goes on?*
- *Are they including doors and windows in ways that keep the enclosure from collapsing?*

Encourage children to build enclosures.

Invite children to use building materials from different areas of the classroom and combine them in their structures. As you visit the building centers, engage children in conversations about what they notice when they combine materials to build enclosures. For example, you might say and ask the following:

- *What happened when you used the cardboard as the floor on this second story?*
- *I noticed that you put Kapla blocks on top of your foam roof. Why?*
- *What do you think would happen if . . .*
  - *these walls were built with the foam blocks instead of these wooden ones?*
  - *this roof were made of unit blocks instead of the cardboard?*
  - *you made a window in this wall?*

When builders use materials of different shapes, sizes, textures, and densities in a single building, they must confront the different effects forces have on the combination of materials. This presents them with opportunities to deepen their understanding of the materials and their characteristics.

Teacher: *What do you think would happen if you added a second story on your dog's house?*

Child: *The roof would crash.*

Teacher: *Why do you say that?*

Child: *It's not strong.*

Teacher: *Show me where it's not strong.*

Encourage children to make representational drawings of their enclosures.

Have paper, markers, and drafting tools available in or next to the building centers. Encourage children to draw their structures during choice time or before cleanup and remind them to look at their structures as they draw. If there are reluctant drawers, use encouraging comments such as the following:

- *What shape is the garage you built? Now draw that shape on your paper. You can do it!*

- *Which part of your house will you draw first: the roof or the foundation?*

Model the process by continuing to draw children's structures. You might establish a routine that involves having children draw their structures just before cleanup a few times each week. When children are ready to share their representational drawings with you, make connections between the details of their structure and their drawings. You might say the following:

- *You told me about the house you built for your cat. Show me the lines on your paper that show the house's walls.*

- *You called the archway in your firehouse the door. Can you show me the door on your drawing?*

- *What shapes did you use in your drawing? Where are those shapes in the house you built?*

- *The blocks in your drawing are tipping to the side. Is that what happened when you built the third story on the house? How did you keep the blocks from tipping over?*

Encourage children to make representational models of their enclosures.

Have glue, tape, scissors, and the collage materials available at a table near the building centers. During choice time, invite a small group of tower builders to the table and introduce the concept of making a model. Together, look at the collage materials and think about which ones might work well to model the kinds of blocks the builders have been using.

Issue: *Aren't my kids too young to draw accurately?*

Response: It is okay if children's drawings don't look like the real thing. What is important is that they are thinking about the characteristics and features of what they are drawing.

Teacher note: When I sat with Tom to talk about his drawing, he said, "I just made my building." I decided to help him connect aspects of his structure to corresponding shapes in his drawing, so I said, "You showed me the chimney on your firehouse. Can you show me the chimney in your drawing?"

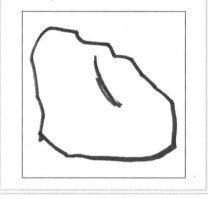

Teacher: *Your drawing shows many upside-down U shapes. Can you show me those shapes in your apartment house?*

It sometimes takes time for children to construct a model of their structures. They might finish work all in one day, or they might work for a few minutes each day during a week.

Children should be able to look at the actual block structure while they construct their model, but if this isn't possible, take a photograph of the original block structure and have it available during the model making.

When children are ready to share the models, look for ways to make connections between their block structures and their models (just like when they share their drawings). You might say the following:

- *I noticed you used this small piece of cardboard for the wall of your model. Do you think it works better than the blocks you used to build the castle? Why do you say that?*

- *I remember how hard you worked to make the door in your waffle block garage so that two motorcycles could fit inside. When you made this model of the garage from cardboard, you didn't have any trouble making the door big enough. Why do you think that is?*

Create a documentation panel.

Use your photographs, sketches, and notes as well as children's work to create a documentation panel of children's experiences building enclosures. You might focus the panel on the strategies they are developing to build stable walls, roofs, and multistoried buildings, or you might focus the panel on the ways they incorporate windows and doors into their enclosures. (See p. 92 for more information on creating documentation panels.) Now is a good time to create and post a panel to let families know about children's focus on enclosures. Include a statement about how children are using their inquiry skills to learn about building stable enclosures.

You will need the panel to focus children's thinking on the strategy and material choices they make to build sturdy enclosures during the upcoming science talks.

REFLECT

Facilitate a walkabout and a science talk every week for five to ten minutes.

Conduct a large group walkabout.

At the end of choice time, gather the whole group together for a walkabout to share and discuss children's enclosures. As builders share their enclosures, help them reflect on the strategies they used. You might ask the following:

ISSUE: *I don't have time to gather collage materials.*

RESPONSE: Send a letter home to families and ask them to save dry and clean food boxes, paper towel rolls, aluminum foil, and other assorted items to send into the classroom for the model-making table.

TEACHER NOTE: I'm going to combine photos of my children's pet houses with their drawings and the photographs I have of the models they've made. I want to make a documentation panel that will tell the story of the way they used Unifix cubes to measure their pets and then build appropriately sized houses.

TEACHER NOTE: During our walkabout, Ivan stood on the roof of his waffle-block house to prove how strong it was. We noticed that he chose to stand on the corner. The middle section was popping apart.

- *What kind of building is this? Have you ever seen or been in one like it?*
- *How did you build it? What happened when you put the roof on?*
- *How strong do you think the roof is? Why do you say that?*

Conduct a science talk focused on characteristics of materials.

Gather the whole group in a circle for a science talk at least once a week and for the next two weeks. Help children share the theories they're developing about how materials' characteristics affect their enclosure's stability. Bring a few of each kind of the blocks children have been building with to the science talk and show them to the children. Share photos of enclosures that were built with a combination of different kinds of blocks.

Focus the science talk on characteristics of materials with a question such as the following:

- *Which blocks are best for building big houses? Why do you think so?*
- *Which blocks are best for building strong walls? Big roofs? Strong roofs? How did you find that out?*

Use follow-up questions such as the following:

- *What was good about using foam blocks?*
- *How did you keep your [structure] from collapsing? Can you show us?*
- *I noticed that you used the rectangle-shaped blocks to make the walls. What do you think might have happened if you used these square ones instead?*
- *Why do you think the cardboard makes a better roof than the long unit blocks?*
- *If I want to build an office building with lots of windows in it, which blocks do you think I should use? Why do you say that? Can you show me how?*

Write children's ideas down on the "What We Know about Building Enclosures" chart and encourage them to find out more about which blocks make the best roofs, second-story floors, and the best walls during choice time throughout the week.

Conduct a science talk focused on design and stability.

Once a week for the two weeks after your group has discussed characteristics of materials, focus science talks on design and stability by sharing children's enclosures. If you can't keep the enclosures standing for your science talks, consider sharing sketches or photographs of the enclosures.

ISSUE: *When I bring my children together for a science talk to discuss the ways they are using different materials to build enclosures, all they want to talk about are the play scenarios they developed to go with their enclosures.*

RESPONSE: Block play invites dramatic play. Try using children's stories to bring up questions about the different building materials they used.

After Essence shared this photo with the group and talked about its parts, his teacher focused the science talk on design and stability.

Teacher: *Which part of your clubhouse do you think has the strongest roof? Why do you say that?*

Invite the builders to talk about their enclosures. Then focus the conversation on design and stability by asking questions such as the following:

- *What shapes do you think make the best roofs?*
- *What do you do to keep the roofs you build from falling in?*

Use follow-up questions such as the following:

- *How do you build your walls?*
- *How do you build your corners?*
- *How do you build the roof?*

Bring some blocks to the science talk and invite children to demonstrate their building strategies.

Wrapping Up

Children have had many experiences building towers and enclosures with different kinds of materials. They have drawn, modeled, discussed, and read about structures. There are many ways you can help children reflect on and celebrate their explorations. As children share their experiences with each other and with their families, they will gain a deeper understanding of the concepts and inquiry skills that have been central to their exploration.

CORE EXPERIENCES

☐ Plan ways to share the building structures exploration with families and friends.

☐ Host an open house.

PREPARATION

☐ Check with your staff and administration, and identify a date for hosting an hour-long open house to share children's building experiences.

☐ Ask children to decorate invitations for families and friends.

☐ Collect the charts, documentation panels, graphs, class books, observational drawings, models, and other documents you and the children created during "Building Structures." Display them, along with children's favorite structure books, around the classroom.

SCHEDULE

☐ 5–10 minutes for a planning meeting a few days before the open house, and again for about an hour before for the open house

The open house described in this step is only one way to bring closure to "Building Structures." You can also help children share and reflect on their building experiences by doing one or more of the following:

- Invite children to take turns bringing home and sharing any class books you've written while they were building structures.

- Display children's drawings and collages in the school's lobby.

- Post all of your documentation panels around the classroom and revisit a few each day during meetings with the whole class. Ask children what they remember about each experience.

MATERIALS

☐ Make a guest book for family and friends to write their comments at the open house.

TEACHING PLAN

ENGAGE

Introduce the open house in a meeting with the whole group for five to ten minutes.

Help children plan for the open house.

Gather your group together. Explain that you would like to plan an open house so they can share with their families and friends some of the things they've done and learned about building structures. Ask the children what they would like to build with their guests. Record their ideas, using words and pictures, on a chart.

Discuss the role of "host."

Help children anticipate what the open house will be like and how they can act as hosts. Together, list the many things children can do with their guests:

- Build at one of the centers.
- Read or look through any of the structure books that have been placed around the classroom.
- Look at documentation panels, class books, journals, representational drawings, models, and so on.
- Make a representational drawing or model of one of their structures.

Involve children in helping you set up the classroom for the open house.

CONDUCT THE BUILDING STRUCTURES OPEN HOUSE

As you welcome guests, point out the guest book. Ask them to write a comment about what they do and see during the open house before they leave. Invite guests to build with the children and point out the various building areas in the classroom. Have children teach the guests how to make representational drawings and models of their buildings. Invite guests to read with children.

TEACHER NOTE: My children love to make invitations and they decided to decorate the invitations with drawings of structures

TEACHER NOTE: Together we generated a list of ideas and challenges for our guests to try at the open house. These are some of the children's suggestions:

- make a cardboard tower as tall as you!
- use unit blocks to make something that looks like a brick wall.
- use Kapla blocks to make a triangular-shaped tower and a square-shaped tower.

PARENT'S COMMENTS

I think it was very interesting to see the children showing what they know. They also seem to enjoy working with the blocks.

extension activities

As children explore, you can enrich and broaden their experiences and learning by taking trips; introducing them to engineers, architects, or builders; and sharing relevant books and videos. The extension activities described below should not become substitutes for children's building explorations. Rather, they should complement these explorations.

We suggest that you do an extension activity about once a week during focused exploration.

Take a Field Trip or a Walk around the Neighborhood

Finding opportunities to connect what is happening in the classroom to the outside world adds meaning to the inquiry. Looking at buildings with children motivates and informs their building work. It provides opportunities to compare and contrast buildings in the neighborhood to the ones children are building in the classroom. It also introduces children to new design features and vocabulary.

Suggested Destinations

- Buildings in the neighborhood
- Town halls, indoor gymnasiums, auditoriums, or other large buildings
- Buildings under construction

Preparation

- If you are going to walk around the neighborhood, do it once ahead of time. Note any safety issues you and the children will

Plan to repeat visits if possible. This will give children opportunities to develop their understanding of design and materials characteristics by allowing them to look at the same structures from different points of view at different stages in their explorations.

need to be aware of, including traffic, broken glass, poison ivy, and so on. Also, note interesting structural features in buildings and plan to point these out to children during the walk.

- If you are going to visit a building such as a gymnasium, auditorium, or the town hall, visit the site ahead of time. Make sure it's a safe place for children to explore. Note interesting structural features in buildings and consider asking the children to sit down and draw some during the trip. If there is a building under construction nearby, consider making regular visits. This is a wonderful opportunity for children to see the actual structure of a building. If you can, invite some of the people working on the building to talk with your children.

BEFORE THE TRIP

- Arrange for adult volunteers to join you on the trip. Plan a time to talk with them about what will happen on the trip, your expectations for what children might engage with, and the ways they can support children's observations at the site. (For example: show volunteers how to use your naturalist tools, and give them a list of questions they can ask to focus children's observations.)

- While children will notice lots of things during the outing, you may want to provide a focus. You might ask the children a question or two and draw out their predictions, recording them in words and pictures. Possible questions include the following:
  - *What kinds of roofs do you think we'll see?*
  - *What kinds of building materials do you think we'll see?*

DURING THE TRIP

Assign small groups of children to each teacher and adult volunteer. Encourage children to act as builders. Invite them to do the following:

- Observe closely.

- Name the building materials.

- Describe the different shapes and kinds of roofs, walls, or special features (balconies, chimneys, and so on).

- Record some observations by making drawings.

Document what children do, say, and see so you can help them discuss and reflect on the visit later in the classroom. If you have a camera, take pictures of children making their observations, as well as the buildings you stop to look at.

AFTER THE TRIP

Have a brief conversation about what you saw. Ask questions such as the following:

- What did you like best about the visit?
- What did you see? Hear? Smell?
- What was special about the place we visited?

Put out drawing and art materials. Encourage children to represent their trip. Write down excerpts from their stories.

The next day, or when your photos have been developed, use children's representational drawings, videotapes, audiotapes, or photos and documentation panels as reflection tools to discuss the question on which you focused children's observations during the visit. Probe children's reflective thinking with questions such as the following:

- *What did you notice about this building?*
- *What do you think makes it strong?*
- *What do you think the builder did to make those windows?*
- *How do you think the builders got the roof to stay up?*
- *How is it the same as the ones you build? How is it different?*

Record children's ideas, in drawings and words, on a chart.

Invite Guests into the Classroom

Children's interest is piqued by visitors. When you introduce children to an adult who thinks about how buildings are constructed, you provide them with a powerful role model as well as an immediate resource.

PREPARATION

- Send home a letter asking family members if they, or anyone they know, would be available to share an expertise, hobby, or interest related to the young builder exploration.
- Talk with the guest ahead of time and describe the kinds of explorations your children have been doing, their interests, and their questions. Suggest the guest bring any tools she uses to show the children. Ask if she minds being videotaped.

SUGGESTED GUESTS

- An architect
- A structural engineer
- A builder

- A mason
- An amateur carpenter

BEFORE THE VISIT

Have a brief conversation with your class about what your visitor does, and ask children what they might want to learn from their guest. Write down children's questions to share with the visitor. The children may want to know more personal things such as where they live or if they have children. These questions are also important to children because they help them see the visitors as real people who use science inquiry in their daily lives.

DURING THE VISIT

Ask the visitors to talk about what they do, and invite them to share journals, tools, books, and stories related to their work as you refer to children's questions. Give children a chance to ask additional questions. Share their standing structures, representational drawings, and classroom books. Ask for comments and suggestions for further study.

AFTER THE VISIT

Have a brief conversation with your class. Ask children what they learned from the visitor and refer to the video of the visit, if one was made. During choice time on the following day, invite children to join you at a small table to draw pictures about the visit for a class book. Ask children about their drawings and write their words down. Consider inviting your guest back in a few weeks. A repeat visit will give children opportunities to ask more focused questions, and they can share the work they do between visits with an adult who shares their interest in building.

Use Books and Videos to Extend the Exploration

There are endless numbers of books and videos that deal with construction. Some entertain, some inform, some inspire. The books that inform a building study need to be scientifically accurate, engaging, and informative for young children. As children move in and out of open and focused exploration, teachers can offer resources in a variety of ways to support the inquiry.

BOOKS

- Books should be integral to children's work and play, and they need to be accessible. Stories, photos, diagrams, poems, lists, and informative text each offer something unique to the process. Make a special effort to display books that have engaging pic-

TEACHER NOTE: Elaine knows Phil, an architect, and she invited him to talk to us about what an architect does. He introduced some basic drawing tools and showed us blueprints. The children were fascinated.

tures of skyscrapers, towers, and interesting enclosures. Encourage children to visit the book corner to look through these books, and encourage other adults to read to small groups or individual children.

- Recommended books to use with extension activities appear in "Books and Web Sites" (p. 82). Use the guidelines presented below and in the section on books and videos to help you choose an assortment of books. In addition to having library books around the classroom, you can use different kinds of books for extension activities in different ways.

FICTION

- Fact and fantasy
- Real life

Choose books that present or raise questions about how buildings are designed to stay standing. Then, when you read aloud each book to an individual child, a small group, or the whole group, you'll be providing a new opportunity for children to wonder about the book's setting, learn vocabulary, and focus their thinking on physical science concepts without disturbing the flow of the story. You might raise issues or ask questions, such as the following:

- *What kind of foundation did the builders make?*
- *How did they get the roof to stay up?*
- *What do you think was the hardest part for the builders to build? Why do you say that?*

NONFICTION

- Information books—Use information books with small groups during choice time to motivate further building and to inform children about different design features and building techniques.
- Image books—Use image books with a few children at a time, so everyone can see. Read aloud or summarize short pieces of text in response to children's interests and questions. Connect the information to children's block play with questions such as the following:
  - *How is this castle like the one you're building?*
  - *This pyramid has secret tunnels inside it. How might you make secret tunnels in the pyramid you're building?*

Preview a variety of these kinds of books (see "Books and Web sites," p. 82, for more information) and choose those that have clear images of different kinds of structures.

BIOGRAPHY

As you read biographies about engineers, architects, or builders aloud, look for opportunities to discuss the characters' passion for building, any obstacles they might have had to overcome to pursue their passion, and the ways they used tools. You might ask questions such as the following:

- *What do you think she wanted to build the most? Why do you say that?*

- *Why do you think his mom gave him the drawing tools? What makes you say that?*

POETRY

Poets write about buildings in a variety of ways: some describe the way they look; some the ways they're used; others focus on the people who live and work in them. Read aloud a variety of poems and ask questions that help children connect their experiences to those expressed in the poetry, such as the following:

- *That poem was about the Statue of Liberty. What words did the poet use to help us see the shapes in the Statue of Liberty?*

- *What words would you add to tell more about how it was made?*

VIDEOS

- Videos that stimulate children's exploration and raise questions for them can be integrated into their work and play. Preview an assortment of videos. In short, they should be scientifically accurate, not too complicated, engaging, and without advertisements.

- Preview videos and choose pieces that feature the kinds of structures children have been building, or ones they can easily compare to those in the local environment. View an excerpt or two with children. If the audio track is too sophisticated or unrelated to your exploration, mute it and focus children on the images. Ask questions that help children wonder about what they're viewing. Encourage them to compare the images to their own experiences.

- Play a video more than once. We often see different things a second or third or fourth time.

resources

Science Teaching

YOUNG CHILDREN'S INQUIRY

"Young Children's Inquiry" is a framework to help you think about how new knowledge is created in science. (See the chart on the following page.) It is useful whether you think about the inquiry of a scientist, your own inquiry, or the inquiry of a child. The framework suggests that the stages follow one another. To some extent they do, but the many arrows suggest that the process of inquiry is not linear, and children will move back and forth and around as they explore the world around them.

Inquiry is about questions, but it's hard for children to ask questions about something if they haven't had a chance to get to know the thing or the materials or the event, whether it is balls rolling, snails, or water flow. So the first stage in the framework is to *engage, notice, wonder,* and *question*—it is a time for children to play, to see what they already know, to mess about in a rich environment with little direct guidance or structure. As children explore, they ask questions through words or actions. As they continue, they may be

struck by a particular idea or question such as "I wonder what would happen if I put this block here?" or "Why is the snail on the wall?"

Many of the questions children raise may not be ones that are possible or interesting to investigate. "Why is the sky blue?" cannot be explored directly. "What is the name of this plant?" will not go far. But "What are ways I can get the water to move?" is the start of a rich investigation. At this stage, children often need adult guidance to begin to *focus observations* and *clarify questions.* They need to be encouraged to make some predictions and guesses about what might happen.

When children engage in more focused explorations, they are entering the experimental phase of inquiry. Even very young children, given the right materials and teacher support and guidance, can *plan, predict, and take action; observe closely; collect, record, and represent experiences and data; reflect on experience; explore patterns and relationships; and construct reasonable explanations and ask new questions.* Notice that on the framework, this process goes around and around. Children may explore a question for a long time. Their explorations may lead to new questions and new investigations.

When children have a good deal of experience and begin to form some ideas, they need to be encouraged to step back from the investigative work, review and reflect on what they have done, and *share, discuss, and reflect with the group, as well as formulate ideas and theories.* By sharing, children have opportunities to reflect and relate their ideas and experiences to what others have done. Differences in experience may demand a return to the exploration. New questions may come up, leading to new explorations.

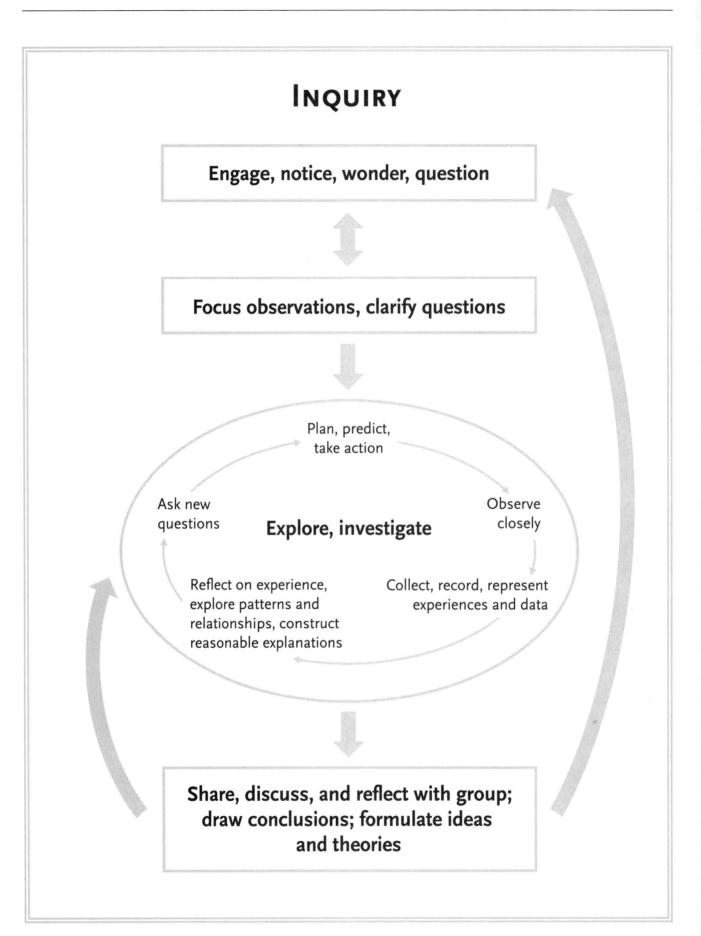

INQUIRY

Engage, notice, wonder, question

Focus observations, clarify questions

Plan, predict,
take action

Ask new
questions

Explore, investigate

Observe
closely

Reflect on experience,
explore patterns and
relationships, construct
reasonable explanations

Collect, record, represent
experiences and data

**Share, discuss, and reflect with group;
draw conclusions; formulate ideas
and theories**

THE TEACHER'S ROLE

Teachers play a number of major roles when exploring science with children. This section includes such responsibilities as the following:

- Create a science-rich environment
- Engage children in science explorations
- Focus and deepen children's experiences and thinking

Observing and assessing, which is also important, will be described in the next section.

CREATE A SCIENCE-RICH ENVIRONMENT

One of the most important roles you play in this exploration is creating an environment and culture that supports and encourages children to build and reflect—your classroom must convey the excitement and wonder of building and learning about stability, design, and characteristics of building materials. Giving children multiple opportunities to explore a variety of building materials is critical, so that children can develop a foundation of experiential knowledge about the ways different materials respond when they are used for building. You can also create a science-rich environment in your own classroom. Displaying interesting posters, picture books, and information books about structures around your classroom allows children to learn more about the designs and materials used to build all kinds of structures.

Organizing and placing materials for building and representation (such as markers, paper, clipboards, and clay) so children have easy access to them and can return them independently will encourage ongoing building and representation. Charts, documentation panels, children's drawings, and posters of buildings displayed at children's eye level help children build on previous explorations, while sparking new ones. Check your environment periodically to see what changes are needed to make your environment reflect the progress of the exploration. For example, are there new materials to add? Which children's work samples and documentation panels should be put away, and which should be added? Which new books reflect children's current interests about buildings and could enrich their experiences?

Children also need time to explore. You may need to adjust your classroom schedule so children can build with different materials several times a week over time. Also be sure to schedule a science talk with the whole class at least once a week so children can share their experiences and ideas, and learn from the experiences of others. You will also need to develop a few simple classroom rules for keeping the building materials organized. (For more information about creating a science-rich environment, see "Getting Ready" on p. 13 and the "Classroom Environment Checklist" on p. 90.)

ENGAGE CHILDREN IN SCIENCE EXPLORATIONS

WHAT CHILDREN ARE DOING: As children move into the open exploration, some will be immediately excited by the ideas and challenges. Others will be more reluctant, perhaps shuffling blocks for a minute or so before moving onto another activity.

TEACHER ROLE: Spend time with those children who are ready to build structures. You do not need to push those who are not engaged. Some will be drawn in by your enthusiasm and the excitement of their peers. You might partner children who are excited about the exploration with children who are less engaged. For example, you might say, "Teresa, can you and Ben build a house for your cat?" Try sharing some good picture books as well. Looking at a book about castles, for example, might draw some children into the exploration. (See "Books and Web Sites" on p. 82.)

As children build, sit with them and observe. Children who are deeply involved with their work are best left to do so. You need to observe and take notes. Through their actions you get clues about what problem they may be trying to solve and what questions they may be asking. These observations will help you guide later discussions and reflection. If children are ready to talk and listen, you might describe what children are doing and seeing. For instance, "You used the rectangular blocks to build the foundation. I don't think your dinosaurs will be able to break into that building!" Also encourage children to share their observations in words and actions, such as using words or their bodies to describe the size of their building. Instead of correcting children's ideas, use words, pictures, drawings, and more direct experiences to encourage children to consider their ideas in new ways. By bringing in resources and offering new experiences, children can explore and refine their ideas.

FOCUS AND DEEPEN CHILDREN'S EXPERIENCES AND THINKING

As children pursue their exploration of structures, you will have many opportunities to push their thinking and their ideas. These opportunities will arise as children engage in conversations, as children represent and document their work, as you use resources, and as you document children's ideas and experiences.

Conversations

As children explore structures, listen to their conversations with each other. Talk with children informally and during weekly large group discussions about their experiences, observations, and ideas.

Communication with Other Children

WHAT CHILDREN ARE DOING: As children work side by side, their conversations with one another push them to put words to their actions and communicate some of their thinking. Their questions of one another may challenge and extend what they are doing and intrigue them with new inquiries. Their debates and arguments will push them to think more about their own ideas and those of others.

TEACHER ROLE: Children's conversations are likely to be very different from those guided by an adult. They are likely to be more directly tied to their fantasies, rules of the game, and requests for help. Your role is to listen carefully and document what may be useful for later discussions and reflection.

Discussions with Children

WHAT CHILDREN ARE DOING: As children are engaged in their work they may welcome interactions with the adults around them. Discussion can raise new questions and suggest new investigations, while helping them to develop their abilities to communicate about their work and thought.

TEACHER ROLE: Engaging children in conversation as they work must be done carefully and only after spending some time observing them. It is best not to interrupt children unless they want to talk, and conversations should be about what they are doing and thinking. Good questions to get started include descriptive ones: "Can you tell me about what you are building? Have you seen one like it?" "How big are you going to make it?" Further discussion can probe more deeply and focus on science concepts. "Why do you think the roof fell in? What do you think is going to happen when you add that block?"

Science Talks

WHAT CHILDREN ARE DOING: During science talks, children share their experiences and their thinking; listen to those of others; and try to make connections between what they have been doing, what others have been doing, and what they already know. It also is a time for children to struggle with new ideas and theories as old ways of understanding are challenged by new experiences.

TEACHER ROLE: Science talks are a critical part of science teaching and learning, helping children to communicate and reflect on their experiences and ideas and to focus their thinking on the science concepts and processes. Your role is to draw out children's ideas and experiences and to challenge their thinking. During your discussions, maintain a focus on the process and substance while encouraging children to tell and dramatize their stories. Use children's representations, your own documentation, and books as a springboard for these discussions: "Here's a picture of the house you built. Can you tell us about it?" "Here's a picture of the tower you built. Can you use your body to show us how tall it was?" Further discussion can probe more deeply, helping children to compare and reflect on their experiences and ideas: "How is the foam block tower different from the unit block one?" "Will thinks Kapla blocks make the best towers because they are lightweight. Maxine, what do you think? How do you know?"

Discussions with a small group are easier to manage than large groups, but the science talks with a large group are important as well, so that children can hear about the ideas and experiences of many others. Begin slowly; start with five- to ten-minute science talks with a large group and increase the time as children's engagement increases. Be sure that all children who want to contribute have a chance to do so. Provide physical props to support children who are less verbal, and use your records to support those who are reluctant to speak out. For example, you might display a collage representation of a house a child made and say, "Kerry, tell us about your house. Can you point to the roof?" Such discussions may encourage children to try new things and question their thinking.

Representation and Documentation

WHAT CHILDREN ARE DOING: When children document or represent their work in various media, they think about their experiences in new ways. Drawing a picture of the garage she built will often prompt a child to observe more closely and highlight details. Or using their bodies to show how much space the roof of their palace was able to span can help children think more deeply about how the roof was constructed.

TEACHER ROLE: It is critical for you to make available materials for children's documentation and representation and to provide space for work and display. But your role goes beyond making materials available. You will need to encourage children to document and represent their work on a regular basis, even if some are reluctant. You may do this by working with them, having them work in pairs, providing notebooks, and celebrating what gets done. Children's documentation and representation also may be the focus of individual or group discussions. Ask a child to describe her work; invite children to use their work in class discussions; probe children's thinking by asking them to tell you why they did something a particular way. "Tell me about your drawing. I noticed you drew this long line here. Where is that part of your structure? What are you trying to show?" "I noticed you drew the roof. So what do you think is holding up the roof? "

Using Resources

WHAT CHILDREN ARE DOING: Children learn about forces and characteristics of materials through building structures that are tall or have roofs. However, direct building is not the only way children can learn about stability, balance, and characteristics of materials. Children's experiences can be enriched by providing additional resources that help them think more deeply about how structures are built.

TEACHER ROLE: Use resources—such as books, field trips, and guest experts—to enrich explorations of building structures. Be sure to display books that have engaging pictures of buildings so children can compare the illustrations to their own constructions. A walk around the block or visits to tall buildings or ones with expansive roofs, and so on, encourage children to compare and contrast actual buildings to those they have been building. Guest experts can provide new information about building materials, designs, and building-related jobs, which can lead to new questions and investigations.

Document Children's Ideas and Experiences

WHAT CHILDREN ARE DOING: As children engage in their explorations, they are certainly thinking about many things. Their actions are the outward reflection of those thoughts. Observing and documenting what children do and say can help you understand their ideas and questions. While young children have many ideas, they tend to focus on the present. Without support they may see experiences as somewhat isolated events and are not always aware of the development of an idea, an experience, or a project. It is also difficult for them to record and keep track of all the data they are gathering. The products of ongoing documentation can be used to provide many opportunities for children to revisit the process and progress of their work and reflect on their understanding.

TEACHER ROLE: Your role is to be the documenter. You can document children's work and the data they are gathering from their exploration in many ways— videotape and audiotape; anecdotal records; photographs; and lists of predictions, observations, and questions. You can then use this documentation to help children revisit, build on, and reflect on their data, ideas, and observations. For example, by going over your notes about children's questions, you will be able to guide them in reflecting on what they found out over time and what ideas they have developed about balance, stability, and characteristics of materials. Documentation panels play a significant role in children's science explorations. It is your role to create a sequence of photos, sketches, science-related conversations, lists of predictions and observations, or children's work with brief annotations that allow children to "replay" and reflect upon what they have done and what has happened. Use the panels as a springboard for stimulating discussions, reenactments, and further explorations. (See "Guidelines for Making Documentation Panels" on p. 92 for more information.)

Observation and Assessment

Observation, documentation, and assessment are critical steps throughout the exploration, helping you gain a picture of children's growing skills and understanding of balance, stability, and characteristics of materials. What children say and do will provide you with important clues about children's understandings; their science inquiry skills (such as their ability to explore, collect data, and so on); and the question they may be asking. Your analysis will help you determine the next steps to take with individual children and the group as a whole. You can also share information about children's science learning with families, your program or school, and funders.

THREE KEY ELEMENTS TO ASSESSMENT

1. Collecting data. Spend at least ten minutes three times a week collecting different kinds of data that captures children's level of engagement and their science understandings. This data can include the following:

   - Written observations that capture what children say and do and wonder about as they explore

   - Photographs, videotapes, and audiotapes that capture children's action and words

   - Samples of children's work that illustrates each child's growing abilities (such as representational drawings and two- or three-dimensional collage representations of structures)

2. Analyzing data regularly. Time spent reflecting on your collection of documents will help you understand the growing skills and understandings of each child in your class. The more kinds of documents you have, the fuller picture you will have of each individual. Examine varied documents reflecting the work of each child, and look across the class to gain a picture of how the group is developing.

3. Drawing conclusions and making decisions. Analysis of the documents you have collected will help you make the important connections between your teaching and the children's learning. Use your analysis of children's growth to consider what your next steps should be with individual children and the group. Who needs encouragement in order to become fully engaged in the explorations? Who is ready for a more complex challenge? Who needs help finding a voice for their observations and ideas? This will be an ongoing process that informs your teaching, helping you refine your approach to teaching science.

A TOOL FOR SCIENCE LEARNING

"Science Outcomes: Science Inquiry Skills and Science Concepts" (p. 97) will tell you what to look for as you analyze your data. This overview of learning goals is organized in two sections: science inquiry skills and science content. For each outcome, it provides three child behaviors sequenced from less to more experienced. These behaviors illustrate how a child might demonstrate their skill or understanding. Use these outcomes and behaviors to help you focus children's science learning and to assess their growth.

TOOLS FOR COLLECTING AND ORGANIZING YOUR DATA

The following three tools will help you document children's inquiry skills and their growing understanding of the science concepts.

1. Observation Record. This form provides a structure and format for recording your observations of children's building explorations. Place copies of the form strategically around the room so you can jot down your observations throughout the day. Use the observation and documentation section of each step of the teaching plan to focus on science concepts and inquiry outcomes as you complete the form. See the sample form on the next page.

2. Document Annotations. Use this form to annotate photos, work samples, transcripts, or any other documents that you may have. When filling out the form, highlight what the document reveals about children's inquiry skills and their understanding of science concepts. Then attach your annotation to each document. The time you take to identify the significant science in each document will help you when it comes time to analyze children's growth and draw conclusions about your teaching. See the sample on the next page.

3. Learning Record. This record provides a format for collecting and analyzing the information you have collected about each child. Note that the content and inquiry items are the same as on the chart "Science Outcomes: Science Inquiry Skills and Science Concepts." Begin a learning record for each child as soon as you start to review your collected observations and documents. Note the evidence you have from observations, conversations, and work samples. Use dates to refer to

OBSERVATION RECORD

Children's Names	Seen and Heard
Danya	• Builds verticals directly on rug and blocks fall • Constructs unit block foundation *then* adds verticals—"That's a floor!"
Ari	• Stacks foam until tower *almost* topples—counts to 12 • Tower falls; "Oh, well." Rebuilds, aligning more carefully and counts 15!

DOCUMENT ANNOTATION

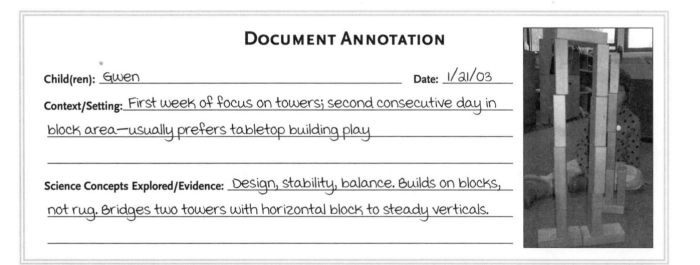

Child(ren): Gwen   Date: 1/21/03

Context/Setting: First week of focus on towers; second consecutive day in block area—usually prefers tabletop building play

Science Concepts Explored/Evidence: Design, stability, balance. Builds on blocks, not rug. Bridges two towers with horizontal block to steady verticals.

specific documents. Add to the records regularly. Your goal is to have a statement about each outcome for each child by the end of the exploration. Note where you find the gaps in information, and plan to focus on engaging those children. At the end of the exploration, check the appropriate box in the child growth column. See the sample on the next page.

Building Materials

When children have opportunities to use and become familiar with buildings made of various materials—as well as size, shape, texture, weight, and flexibility—

they learn about the different ways one characteristic of a building material can affect its ability to be stacked and balanced. Provide children with a wide variety of materials to use as they build and represent. Some materials can be collected for low or no cost while others can be purchased from supply stores.

See "Getting Ready, Step 3: Preparing the Physical Environment: Materials and Resources," p. 16, for a detailed list of suggested classroom materials.

LOW- TO NO-COST MATERIALS

There are a few ways you can find free or very inexpensive materials for the classroom.

LEARNING RECORD

Child: Denise

Science Inquiry Skills	Child Growth	Evidence
Explores/questions	☐ Emerging ☐ Sometimes ☒ Consistently	3/12 builds unit block house 4/5 combines Kapla and foam to make layered tower
Begins to investigate	☐ Emerging ☒ Sometimes ☐ Consistently	3/22 stacks Kapla on flat sides—wiggles table to see if they fall
Collects data	☐ Emerging ☒ Sometimes ☐ Consistently	4/10 counts blocks in tower 5/13 puts toy dog in house to see if it's big enough

- Ask families to save and donate clean, empty food boxes, and paper towel and toilet paper tubes.

- Call businesses and ask them to donate clean cardboard or foam to the school. Some lumber-yards will give you pieces of wood, which may need to be sanded to avoid splinters.

- Many communities have recycling centers that collect and organize materials you can purchase for a small price.

Try to find different kinds of foam pieces, some that are very squishy and some that are firm. Also, look for different kinds of lightweight cardboard, some with a smooth surface and some with a rougher texture. Before you know it, you will develop an "eye" for picking out materials that will engage children in additional building explorations.

PURCHASED MATERIALS

The basic materials you need to provide for children's exploration include a large set of unit blocks, two or three large sets of small-scale blocks, a large set of foam blocks, books, and clipboards. In addition, you need basic materials for children's representations.

The chart on page 81 lists some materials that can be purchased, and a few suppliers. Here is the contact information for those suppliers.

COMMUNITY PLAYTHINGS
359 Gibson Hill Road
Chester, NY 10918-2321
800-777-4244
www.communityplaythings.com

DELTA EDUCATION
P. O. Box 3000
Nashua, NH 03061-3000
800-442-5444
www.delta-education.com

DISCOUNT SCHOOL SUPPLY
P. O. Box 7636
Spreckels, CA 93962-7636
800-627-2829
www.discountschoolsupply.com

DR. DREW'S TOYS, INC.
P. O. Box 510501
Melbourne Beach, FL 32951
407-984-1018
Fax: 407-984-9090

BUILDING MATERIAL SOURCES

Materials	Supplier
Unit blocks: Classroom set 150–200 wooden blocks in 10 or more shapes	Discount School Supply; Educational Concepts; Lakeshore Learning Materials
Kapla blocks Set of 200 blocks	Discount School Supply; Kapla USA
Foam blocks 50-plus blocks to a set	Discount School Supply; Lakeshore Learning Materials
Dr. Drew's Discovery Blocks	Dr. Drew's Toys, Inc.
Tabletop blocks Colorful, wooden blocks, about 50 to a set	Discount School Supply; Lakeshore Learning Materials; Learning Materials Workshop
Mini unit blocks 100-plus blocks in 10 or more shapes	Discount School Supply; Educational Concepts
Cube blocks Set of 50 to 100 one-inch cube blocks	Discount School Supply; Delta Education
Straws and connectors Set of 100-plus	Discount School Supply
Cardboard blocks 40–50 in one, two, or three sizes	Discount School Supply
Hollow blocks 20–50 blocks to a set	Discount School Supply; Community Playthings; Lakeshore Learning Materials
Large waffle blocks 18–36 plastic blocks in a set	Lakeshore Learning Materials
Small waffle blocks	Discount School Supply
Flexible wire	J. L. Hammett Co.
Picture books of structures	Bookstores
Toy animals and dollhouse people	Learning Things, Inc.; Discount School Supply
Architectural drawing tools	Lakeshore Learning Materials
Clipboards	Office supply stores

EDUCATIONAL CONCEPTS
70 New River Road
Manville, RI 02838
800-962-6785
www.educoncepts.com

J. L. HAMMETT CO.
P. O. Box 859057
Braintree, MA 02185-9057
800-955-2200
www.hammett.com

KAPLA USA
6719 Rocky Bar Road
Elkton, VA 22827
866-GO-KAPLA
www.kaplausa.com

LAKESHORE LEARNING MATERIALS
2695 East Dominguez Street
Carson, CA 90810
800-778-4456
www.lakeshorelearning.com

LEARNING MATERIALS WORKSHOP
274 North Winooski Avenue
Burlington, VT 05401
800-693-7164
www.learningmaterialswork.com

LEARNING THINGS, INC.
P. O. Box 1112
Olean, NY 14760
800-284-5688
www.learningthings.us

Involving Families

A number of children's family members are likely to have knowledge or abilities that will be valuable as you engage in building structures. Some will be avid builders or will have experience designing structures. Find out which resources exist in your community of families, and try to make use of some family members. These visits enhance both children's learning and the home-school connection.

It will be helpful to set the stage for family support early. At the beginning of the exploration, send home the letter to families (p. 83) with each child to intro-duce families to the exploration. Let them know what children will do and learn, and suggest ways that they can support their children's science learning.

You can also extend children's science learning by suggesting science-related activities for families to do at home and in the community. These activities can reinforce the science children are learning in the classroom and outdoors, while helping children and families see science phenomena in their daily lives. As the exploration progresses, send home "Families Building Structures" (p. 84), which offers building activities that caregivers can do with their children.

Books and Web Sites

It is important to evaluate books, Web sites, and other resources on structures that you select for children to use in the classroom. Select carefully, because the materials that you choose will be valuable resources for the children's explorations. It is important that all resources meet these basic criteria:

- Characters and content should reflect cultural diversity. Not every book and Web site must represent different cultures, but your collection should as a whole.

- Stereotypes should be absent.

- Content should be scientifically accurate.

This list of books is broken into additional subdivisions. Each category contains selection criteria and a set of annotated examples to help you identify high-quality resources. But keep in mind that books go out of print and are not always available. If the examples listed below are not obtainable, use the given criteria to choose others like them. It is best to have different kinds of books and resources available for children to use, and remember that types of books can overlap. For example, *Castle* by David Macaulay can be considered as either an image or an information book.

Finally, there is also a list of resource books and Web sites for teachers that you may find helpful in gathering information about structures and ideas to use in the classroom. Specific Web sites may change; those listed are examples of the kinds of sites that can support the exploration.

Dear Families,

You may have noticed that your children are naturally curious about the world around them. They may especially notice tall buildings or new houses. They may also be interested in building structures in their everyday lives—a home for their stuffed animals, a castle for their dolls, or a fortress for themselves. You may also see them finding joy in knocking these same structures down, or just gazing up at tall buildings with wonder.

As part of our science curriculum this year we are going to study building structures. Your children will develop a scientific approach to their investigation of structures as they focus on building tall structures and enclosures, trying out different building materials, and discovering which materials work best for different kinds of construction.

At school, your children will do the following:

- Build tall structures and enclosures using many different kinds of materials
- Create drawings to represent what they have built
- Research in books to learn more about different kinds of structures
- Share their thinking and ideas

You can really help our explorations by encouraging your children to build at home. There is no need for you to have specific materials—children will delight in building with anything from Popsicle sticks to milk cartons. Lego and Duplo blocks are also popular, but children do not encounter the same challenges in terms of balance and gravity when building with these blocks. Your children will be delighted if, instead, you encourage their explorations and show an interest in their discoveries, and even share your own observations—a new house or building going up in your neighborhood.

We can also use your assistance and expertise at school. If you have time to volunteer, come help us as we explore and build. An extra pair of hands is always welcome. Or if you are knowledgeable about construction, architecture, or anything else related to our study, let us know. We'd love to have you share your experience with all the children.

BOOKS FOR CHILDREN

NONFICTION

Listed below are three different kinds of nonfiction books for children: image books, information books, and biographies. Each of these nonfiction books has at least three criteria in common—scientifically accurate content; detailed illustrations or photographs that give children information and stimulate ideas; and content that is inherently interesting to children, stimulates their exploration, and raises questions for them.

Image Books

Image books for children ages three through five are any books that use large, detailed illustrations or photographs to convey information and inspire children to explore further. These can include books that are specifically written for children or books that are meant for adults or older children but have engaging pictures that inform and stimulate young children's thinking.

Examples of image books include the following:

- Dupré, Judith. 1996. *Skyscrapers*. New York: Black Dog & Leventhal Publishers, Inc.

  This book of skyscraper photographs is brilliant. Not only are the photographs striking, but the book's tall, thin shape draws attention to the main characteristic of skyscrapers—they are tall! It will definitely highlight for children what a skyscraper is and encourage them to build tall.

- Macaulay, David. 2000. *Building Big*. New York: Houghton Mifflin.

  Macauley's detailed illustrations will captivate children's attention as they look at skyscrapers,

FAMILIES BUILDING STRUCTURES

Building with children is fun. And by building together, you and your child
will learn more about each other and the world of structures around you.

Tips for Outdoor Explorations

Take a walk with your child in your city center, a park, or your neighborhood. Bring along clipboards, paper, and pencils so that as you and your child observe, both of you can sketch the structures you see, trying to capture the details.

During your walk, you and your child can note the following:

- Size of structures you see (such as comparing the tallest, the widest, or the one that has the most room inside)

- Materials structures (such as chimneys, foundations, or roofs) are built from

- People who work or live in the structures ("What do they need inside their offices or homes?")

- Ways design features differ (such as looking for arches, pillars, and different kinds of roofs)

- Characteristics of each structure (such as number of windows or doors and their shapes)

- Ways different structures are alike and different

Tips for Indoor Explorations

We suggest you and your child build with materials that do not fit together to make tight connections—for example, use blocks, wood scraps, small cans, and empty boxes filled with sand instead of Duplos, Legos, Brio-Mec, or similar toys.

Tips for Builder Talks

As your child builds with different materials, use these tips to spark some conversations:

- Invite your child to tell you about her structure.

- Help your child think about the characteristics of the structure. ("What are its parts? What is its shape? What is it used for?")

- Help your child think about the characteristics of the building materials. ("How do you think your tower would be different if the cardboard blocks you are using were made of wood? What do you think would happen if this rectangular block was shaped like a triangle instead?")

- Wonder out loud with your child. ("I wonder what might happen if you used the foam blocks to build the foundation. I wonder if we can make this even taller.")

Provide your child with the support he needs to share his thinking:

- Give your child time to think before he responds to your questions and comments. Silent time is okay.

- Find ways for your child to show you what he knows (for example, using his hands to show you how tall his building is).

Avoid comments that could limit your child's thinking, such as the following:

- Explaining the science

- Correcting ideas (rather, ask more questions)

- Moving on too quickly (allow the child to decide when to move on)

bridges, tunnels, and dams. The clear text provides history and details that will get children thinking about the use of different materials and solving design problems. Other Macauley books that address building issues include *Pyramid, Mill, Castle, Cathedral, City, Underground,* and *Unbuilding*.

- Nelson, Peter. 1994. *Treehouses: The Art and Craft of Living Out on a Limb*. New York: Houghton Mifflin.

  This book provides a look at a different kind of structure—the tree house. The structures are fascinating, and the photographs will engage and inspire even the most reluctant builder. By showing structures that are so often part of a child's play, this book may provide some children with an even more direct connection to building structures.

- Steltzer, Ulli. 1999. *Building an Igloo*. New York: Henry Holt.

  This photo essay follows a man and his son as they build an igloo. Each step in the process is accompanied by a photograph, introducing children to this tradition that is part of the Inuit culture.

Information Books

Information books for children ages three through five are books that focus on specific topics, such as skyscrapers, cities, construction, or architects. Or they can be books that focus on specific questions, such as "How is a building built?" or "Who decides what a building will look like?" These books provide children with information that answers questions and raises more questions.

Examples of information books include the following:

- Gibbons, Gail. 1996. *How a House Is Built*. New York: Holiday House.

  This book illustrates how a house is built from beginning to end. It describes how the architect, surveyors, heavy equipment operators, carpenters, plumbers, and landscapers all contribute to the work.

- Hayward, Linda. 2001. *Jobs People Do: A Day in the Life of a Builder*. DK Readers Series. New York: DK Publishing.

  Intended for children who are beginning to read, but can also be read aloud or used as an image book. Clear photographs and simple text make it ideal for young children, as do the picture dictionary boxes that "show" the meanings of words.

- MacDonald, Fiona. 2001. *Homes*. Discovering World Cultures series. New York: Crabtree Publishing Company.

  Introduces children to many different homes from around the world in great detail. Explains why certain homes are built in different cultures and areas of the world, including factors considered when building (such as climate and available materials).

- Wilkinson, Philip. 2000. *Building*. Eyewitness Book Series. New York: DK Publishing.

  Color photographs of houses, towers, and all their components (such as windows, doors, and ceilings) deliver a unique "eyewitness" view into the world of architecture. Provides a wealth of information about how structures are designed and built. Other titles in the series include *Pyramid, Castle,* and *Force and Motion*.

Biographies

Biographies for children ages three through five are real stories about real people. Biographical characters should be related to the topic of study, and the story should be focused and comprehensible enough for children this age. No biographies of building structures written for children in this age range were found; however, some books about well-known architects that children can look at as image books can be helpful and are listed below. Discuss with children how the structures in each book are by a single architect and encourage them to notice similarities and differences in the buildings.

Examples of biographies include the following:

- Jordan, Sandra, and Jan Greenberg. 2000. *Frank O. Gehry: Outside In*. New York: DK Publishing.

  Introduces children to the unusual and remarkable architecture of Frank Gehry. His structures are anything but conventional, and will certainly delight and inspire children to take risks of their own.

- Smith, Kathryn. 1998. *Frank Lloyd Wright: America's Master Architect*. New York: Abbeville Press.

  The photographs in this book will expose children to the architecture of Frank Lloyd Wright. Looking at his graceful buildings, they will get a glimpse of why he is considered one of the greatest architects.

FICTION

Listed below are two different kinds of fiction books for children: fact and fantasy and real-life fiction. Each of the fiction books has at least three of the following criteria in common—developmentally appropriate presentation (rhythm, repetition, story length, vocabulary, font size); content that is inherently interesting to children, stimulates their exploration, and raises questions for them; illustrations that explain the story; and a substantial amount of scientifically accurate content.

Fact and Fantasy

A major feature of fact and fantasy books for children ages three through five is that they should raise questions for children about scientific phenomena and spark their interests. Books that view the world through the eyes of different cultures can help children begin to understand science from different perspectives. While much of the content should be scientifically accurate, these books may also contain some fantasy.

Examples of fact and fantasy books for children include the following:

- Marshall, James. 1996. *The Three Little Pigs.* New York: Puffin.

  This version of the timeless fairy tale combines comical illustrations and witty text to bring the story to life for young children. Focusing on the three different kinds of houses that the pigs build is a nice way to open a discussion with children about the strengths and weaknesses of building with different materials.

- McLerran, Alice. 1991. *Roxaboxen.* New York: Lothrop, Lee & Shepard.

  This is a story about an imaginary town called Roxaboxen. Children use their creativity and imagination to create this town out of rocks, boxes, and desert glass. Colorful illustrations, simple text, and the appeal of fantasy will spark your children's interest in building a town of their own.

- Lowell, Susan. 1992. *The Three Little Javelinas.* Flagstaff, Ariz.: Rising Moon.

  This twist on the classic tale of "The Three Little Pigs" introduces children to javelinas, the southwestern cousin of the pig. This multicultural version has houses made of tumbleweed, saguaro rib, and adobe, with Native American and Latino characters.

Real-Life Fiction

These books differ from other fiction books because, while the story is fictional, the science content is accurate. Where other fiction books might contain bits of fantasy, these do not. Similar to fact and fantasy books, real-life fiction books should also raise questions for children about scientific phenomena.

Examples of real-life fiction books for children include the following:

- Barton, Byron. 1981. *Building a House.* New York: Penguin Books.

  The simple words and pictures in this book follow each step of building a house—the bulldozer digs a hole, bricklayers lay bricks, carpenters make a floor, and so on. Children will see all the different people involved in building a house and what their jobs are, and will learn about the various components such as pipes, wires, and a chimney.

- Cooper, Elisha. 1999. *Building.* New York: Greenwillow Books.

  This book begins with a vacant space and ends with a building. The pictures are simpler than *Building a House*, but the story is more detailed and the text more poetic. (For example, "If a nail has to be pulled out with the claw of the hammer, it screeches as if it were happy right where it was.") Children will enjoy learning how this building is constructed.

POETRY

Poetry for children ages three through five encompasses characteristics of both fiction and nonfiction books. It can be either completely scientifically accurate or contain bits of fantasy and should contain content that is inherently interesting to children, stimulates their exploration, and raises questions for them. Unlike other books for children, however, poetry uses words rather than pictures to illustrate experiences and phenomena, often containing rhyming verses. This does not mean that these books will have no pictures, just that the words will be able to draw a picture themselves.

Examples of poetry books include the following:

- Crosbie, Michael. 2000. *Arches to Zigzags: An Architecture ABC.* New York: Harry N. Abrams, Inc.

  Uses rhymes and full-color photographs to introduce children to different architectural elements. The rhyme for each element ends with a question to spark children's thinking and encourage their exploration. An afterword further explains terms from the book.

- Lewis, Kevin. 2001. *The Lot at the End of My Block.* New York: Hyperion Books.

  This cumulative rhyming tale tells the story of a boy as he watches a building go up in the vacant lot down the street. The brightly colored pictures and repetitive text will hold children's interest as they look through the boy's eyes at the construction vehicles and builders working to erect this structure.

RESOURCE BOOKS AND WEB SITES FOR TEACHERS

These resources should be used only by the teacher to gather information and get ideas to use in the classroom. The main criterion for these resources is that they should contain scientifically accurate content. Although the books will not be used by young children, it may be helpful if they are written simply and clearly so teachers can access information without wading through difficult scientific language. Also be aware that any Web sites listed here might be discontinued. They are listed as examples of the kinds of information available on the Web.

RESOURCE BOOKS

- Education Development Center, Inc. 1997. *Structures.* (A module). Dubuque, Iowa: Kendall Hunt Publishing Co.

  This teacher's guide from Insights: An Elementary Hands-On Inquiry Science Curriculum is developed for the sixth-grade level. While it includes activities that you would not take directly to the classroom, it is useful for teachers as a resource on the science involved in building structures.

- Forman, George, and Karen Hewitt. 1990. *The Learning Materials Workshop Blocks: An Educational Guide.* Burlington, Vt.: Learning Materials Workshop.

  Offers a detailed look at the value of block play in early childhood and gives suggestions for using the Learning Materials Workshop blocks in the classroom.

- Hirsch, Elizabeth, ed. 1996. *The Block Book.* Washington, D.C.: National Association for the Education of Young Children.

  An excellent resource providing a wealth of information about using blocks with young children— a must for any early childhood teacher.

- Wellhousen, Karyn, and Judith Keiff. 2001. *A Constructivist Approach to Block Play in Early Childhood.* Albany, N.Y.: Delmar Publishers.

  This book provides a comprehensive look at how to use building materials with young children.

WEB SITES

- *www.pbs.org/wgbh/buildingbig*

  "Building Big" is a companion to the David Macauley book and videos. The "Wonders of the World Databank" contains information and photographs of different structures all over the world. It also includes an extensive glossary and information about building-related careers, as well as information on *Thinking Big and Building Small*, a video for teachers on the process of engineering design.

- *www.emporis.com/en*

  This site has lots of information and photographs about towers from around the world and the architects who built them. It also includes information on high rises in local cities, including Cleveland, Detroit, Indianapolis, and Houston, which may help some teachers locate buildings to visit on a field trip.

appendices

CLASSROOM ENVIRONMENT CHECKLIST

Classroom Materials Inventory

Complete an inventory of the materials you have for the "Building Structures" exploration by filling in the middle column of the chart below. In the right column, list what you need to obtain. You do not need all of these types of blocks, just a variety (large and small, different textures and materials, and so on). Refer to p. 81 of the teacher's guide for a more complete list of recommended materials.

Item	Inventory	Needs
Unit blocks		
Cardboard blocks		
Hollow blocks		
Kapla blocks		
Dr. Drew blocks		
Large dominoes		
Small-scale unit blocks		
Tabletop blocks		
One-inch cube blocks		
Classic alphabet blocks		
Straws and connectors		
Waffle blocks		

Classroom Environment Checklist (cont'd)

Set Up the Classroom

Complete the chart below to help you plan how your space will reflect your study of building structures. Use the check column on the right to note your accomplishments. See p. 18 in the teacher's guide for specific recommendations.

Recommendations	Plans	✔
Three building areas		
Wall space		
Book space		
Table space for three-dimensional work		
Accessible materials and tool storage		

Plan the Schedule

Two special times for building work are recommended on p. 19 of the teacher's guide: choice time and planning and reflection time. Use the following chart to assess your needs and plan necessary changes to your daily schedule.

Time	Current Schedule	Change in Schedule
Choice time 45–60 minutes of choice time at least three times per week		
Science talk 5–10 minutes as a whole group at least once per week		

GUIDELINES FOR CREATING DOCUMENTATION PANELS

How Do I Make a Documentation Panel?

1. Collect documents.

- Collect related work samples—drawings, paintings, and photos of children's three-dimensional representations.

- Collect dialogue. Record science-related conversations with and among children, jot down a conversation that can be typed up later, or ask children to tell you about their work or a photo.

- Pull together notes and data that have been collected during the exploration—science inquiry charts, a list of predictions, descriptive observations, new questions, and so on.

- If you have access to a camera, take photos of children making science-related observations or working on buildings. Get close-ups of children's hands and faces. Enlarge 3- by 5-inch and 4- by 6-inch photos on a photocopier, or print digital photos on 8- by 11-inch paper (the photos should be large enough for a group of children to view together).

2. Decide the panel's focus.

- Discovery—Children discover the ways different kinds of blocks feel.

- Exploration—Children explore the ways different kinds of blocks respond to being stacked.

- Data collection—Children measure the height of their towers.

- Comparison—Children compare different ways of designing houses.

- Tool use—Children use drafting tools to draw plans of their buildings.

How Do I Put Together the Panel?

1. Arrange your documents in chronological order, from left to right, across the board in a single, straight line. Adhere your photos with a glue stick, rubber cement, or two-sided tape. (White glue wrinkles paper.)

2. Add text to your panel. Suggestions include the following:

- Interview the children whose work is featured on the panel and use some of their words as captions under their work samples.

- Add the question or challenge that guided the children's focused exploration.

- Add the names children give their structures.

3. Add a title that focuses your reading audience on the panel's key message. For example:

- Max supports his castle's roof with cylinder blocks.

- Measuring our towers.

How Can I Display the Panels and Share Them with Families?

- Post the panels at children's eye level. When you run out of wall space, move the ones that aren't currently being used into the hall or to some other location where families and colleagues might enjoy them.

- Invite children to share panels with family members. Post a couple of questions next to the panel to prompt conversation and help focus it on the aspect of science inquiry featured on the panel.

- Share panels during parent conferences. Use them to reflect on specific aspects of children's science experiences and their growth and development.

OBSERVATION RECORD

Teacher_____ Date: _____

Setting:_____

Check one: ☐ Open Exploration   ☐ Focused Exploration

Check one: ☐ Towers   ☐ Enclosures

Step:_____

Children's Names	Seen and Heard

DOCUMENT ANNOTATION

Child(ren): _____   Date: _____

Context/Setting:_____

_____

_____

Science Concepts Explored/Evidence: _____

_____

_____

DOCUMENT ANNOTATION

Child(ren): _____   Date: _____

Context/Setting:_____

_____

_____

Science Concepts Explored/Evidence: _____

_____

_____

DOCUMENT ANNOTATION

Child(ren): _____   Date: _____

Context/Setting:_____

_____

_____

Science Concepts Explored/Evidence: _____

_____

_____

LEARNING RECORD: PART I

Child _____   Birth Date: _____

Date Exploration Begun: _____   Completed: _____

Science Inquiry Skills	Child Growth	Evidence
Engages, notices, wonders, questions	☐ Emerging ☐ Sometimes ☐ Consistently	
Begins to explore, investigate	☐ Emerging ☐ Sometimes ☐ Consistently	
Collects data	☐ Emerging ☐ Sometimes ☐ Consistently	
Records and represents experience	☐ Emerging ☐ Sometimes ☐ Consistently	
Reflects on experience	☐ Emerging ☐ Sometimes ☐ Consistently	
Uses language to communicate feelings	☐ Emerging ☐ Sometimes ☐ Consistently	
Shares, discusses, and reflects with group	☐ Emerging ☐ Sometimes ☐ Consistently	

LEARNING RECORD: PART II

Child _____ Birth Date: _____

Date Exploration Begun: _____ Completed: _____

Science Concepts	Child Growth	Evidence
Forces—Gravity, tension, compression	☐ Emerging ☐ Sometimes ☐ Consistently	
Design, stability, and balance	☐ Emerging ☐ Sometimes ☐ Consistently	
Characteristics of objects children build with	☐ Emerging ☐ Sometimes ☐ Consistently	
Characteristics of materials building objects are made from	☐ Emerging ☐ Sometimes ☐ Consistently	

OUTCOMES CHARTS

The two outcomes charts that follow will help you to describe and record children's progress. You may also find them useful when talking with others about the goals of *Building Structures with Young Children*. The first chart, "Science Outcomes," is in two parts: science inquiry skills and science concepts. Each skill or concept is defined in the column on the left. On the right are three levels of behaviors, starting with simple and moving to more complex. What your children will achieve will depend on their level of maturity and prior experiences.

The second chart is "Connections between Inquiry Skills and Outcomes in Other Domains." This chart provides a visual presentation of how science inquiry skills relate to outcomes or skills in other areas. The inquiry skills are listed in the left-hand column. Language, literacy, and mathematics skills, as well as social abilities and approach to learning, appear at the top. Checked boxes show where inquiry skills support abilities in other areas. While the outcomes of other subject areas listed are based on the Head Start Child Outcomes Framework, they are also relevant to a range of early childhood programs.

SCIENCE OUTCOMES: SCIENCE INQUIRY SKILLS AND SCIENCE CONCEPTS

Science Inquiry Skills	Builder Behaviors
Engages, notices, wonders, questions: Engages in open-ended explorations of structures with a variety of materials; forms questions that guide actions.	• Tries to build; willingly goes to block area or other building centers. • Persists in building; tries to improve upon previous structure with similar materials. • Tries a variety of designs with a variety of materials.
Begins to explore, investigate: Engages in simple investigations to extend previous observations of structures, test predictions, and pursue questions about building.	• Tries to build taller and taller as if asking "What will happen if I add another block?" • Focuses on a specific question that can be answered. ("Can I use big blocks at the top of this structure?") • Designs simple investigations. ("I'm going to try to build a tower taller than you with Kapla blocks.")
Collects data: Uses senses, varied tools, and simple measures to gather data about materials and structures.	• Gathers basic information, using sight and touch. (Realizes that wood blocks are different from foam blocks.) • Attempts basic measurement: Counts numbers of blocks; uses nonstandard comparison. ("It is as tall as me!") • Uses string, paper, tape measures, and other tools to collect quantitative data on structures. ("The tower is as tall as this piece of string.")
Records and represents experience: Describes, records, and communicates experiences and information about building through a variety of means, including two- and three-dimensional representation, charts, and movement.	• Attempts simple line drawings of structures. • Creates two- and three-dimensional representations that incorporate several characteristics of a structure. • Uses materials of different scale to attempt an accurate replica of a structure, such as mini unit blocks or paper-shape cutouts.
Reflects on experience, synthesizes and analyzes data from experiences: Explores patterns and relationships among building experiences; makes reasonable predictions, explanations, and generalizations based on experience.	• Draws on prior experiences when describing, comparing, and talking about building. ("I built a big house like that yesterday.") • Bases predictions and explanations on observations and data from past experiences. ("If you add that block, it's gonna fall!") • Connects observations and data from multiple explorations, identifying patterns and relationships, and stating conclusions. ("The best thing to make big towers with is the Kapla blocks.")
Uses language to communicate findings: Develops increased building and structures vocabulary and ability to communicate observations and ideas.	• Responds to direct questions about characteristics of building materials. • Contributes more detailed descriptions and ideas about personal building. • Mentions various characteristics of different building materials and explains why they were used when they were.

SCIENCE OUTCOMES: SCIENCE INQUIRY SKILLS AND SCIENCE CONCEPTS (CONT'D)

Science Inquiry Skills	Builder Behaviors
Collaborates: Shares materials, tasks, and ideas; collaborates in joint building or other inquiry related to structures.	• Builds alone or alongside others. • Takes part in building with a small group. • Plans, negotiates, and discusses building in a small group.

Science Concepts	Builder Behaviors
Gravity, tension, and compression: Shows a growing awareness of the forces that affect personal building.	• Anticipates that not all buildings will stay up (such as builds until the building falls, then begins again). • Shows awareness that the taller it gets, the harder it is to keep standing (such as placing blocks on a tower with care—as if putting one on incorrectly will cause the tower to fall). • Recognizes that there are several things to keep in mind when building stable structures (such as recognizing that objects at the bottom of buildings might get squished; heavy walls might fall over).
Design, stability, and balance: Shows a growing awareness how materials put together will affect a building's strength.	• Notices that by placing blocks in a certain way, the building can stand better (such as stacking blocks while giving thought about placement). • Begins to move beyond stacking to more sophisticated building (such as making a "bridge" using a supporting post and beam to increase the width of the building). • Begins to show awareness of several new strategies while making more intricate structures (such as adds support to foundations to make them more stable; buttresses heavy walls by adding external supports; makes parts of straw structures to add to existing ones).
Characteristics of materials with which children build: The child shows a growing awareness of the different characteristics (shape, size, texture) of materials they are building with and how those characteristics affect their buildings.	• Begins to show awareness that different objects have different properties (such as size, texture, shape, and color). • Notices that when building with blocks, certain shapes work best in certain places. • Becomes more intentional about the building (such as choosing blocks because of their shapes or size).
Characteristics of materials of which buildings or structures are made: Develops an awareness of the different characteristics of the building materials (such as wood, foam, or plastic) and how these characteristics affect their building; shows an increasing awareness of the different characteristics (such as hardness, flexibility, or weight) of the materials buildings or structures are made of and how these characteristics affect them.	• Notices that the objects used for building are made of different materials (such as some blocks are made from wood, some from foam). • Notices that different materials respond differently in different parts of a structure (such as wood on top of foam "pushes it down"). • Shows awareness that different materials suit different building needs; is more intentional (such as foam blocks, because they are light, can be used more easily at the top of a structure).

CONNECTIONS BETWEEN INQUIRY SKILLS AND OUTCOMES IN OTHER DOMAINS

LANGUAGE **and** **SCIENCE**	Shows progress in understanding and following simple and multistep directions.	Shows increasing abilities to understand and use language to communicate information, experience, ideas, feelings, opinions, questions, and so on.	Progresses in abilities to initiate and respond appropriately in conversation and discussions with peers and adults.	Links new learning experiences and vocabulary to what is already known about a topic.
Explores/questions—Engages in open-ended explorations; forms questions that guide actions.		✓	✓	
Begins to investigate—Engages in simple investigations to extend observations, test predictions, and pursue questions.	✓	✓	✓	✓
Collects data—Uses senses, varied tools, and simple measures to gather data.	✓	✓		
Records and represents experience—Describes and records experiences and information through a variety of means, including two- and three-dimensional representation, charts, and movement.		✓		✓
Synthesizes and analyzes data from experiences—Sees patterns in data and relationships among experiences; makes reasonable predictions, explanations, and generalizations based on experience.		✓	✓	✓
Uses language to communicate findings—Develops increased vocabulary and ability to communicate observations and ideas.		✓	✓	✓
Collaborates—Shares materials, tasks, and ideas; collaborates in joint investigations.		✓	✓	

CONNECTIONS BETWEEN INQUIRY SKILLS AND OUTCOMES IN OTHER DOMAINS (CONT'D)

LITERACY and SCIENCE	Progresses in abilities to retell and dictate stories from books or experiences, act out stories in dramatic play, and predict what will happen next in a story.	Develops an understanding that writing is a way of communicating for a variety of purposes.	Begins to represent stories and experiences through pictures, dictation, and play.	Experiments with a growing variety of writing tools, such as pencils, crayons, and computers.
Explores/questions—Engages in open-ended explorations; forms questions that guide actions.				
Begins to investigate—Engages in simple investigations to extend observations, test predictions, and pursue questions.	✓			
Collects data—Uses senses, varied tools, and simple measures to gather data.		✓		✓
Records and represents experience—Describes and records experiences and information through a variety of means, including two- and three-dimensional representation, charts, and movement.	✓	✓	✓	✓
Synthesizes and analyzes data from experiences—Sees patterns in data and relationships among experiences; makes reasonable predictions, explanations, and generalizations based on experience.	✓	✓	✓	✓
Uses language to communicate findings—Develops increased vocabulary and ability to communicate observations and ideas.	✓	✓	✓	✓
Collaborates—Shares materials, tasks, and ideas; collaborates in joint investigations.				

CONNECTIONS BETWEEN INQUIRY SKILLS AND OUTCOMES IN OTHER DOMAINS (CONT'D)

MATHEMATICS and SCIENCE	Begins to recognize, describe, compare, and name common shapes and their parts and attributes.	Increases understanding of directionality, order, positions of objects, and words (*up, down, over, under, top, bottom,* and so on).	Enhances abilities to recognize, duplicate, and extend simple patterns using a variety of materials.	Increases abilities to match, sort, put in a series, regroup, and compare objects according to one or two attributes (such as shape or size).	Shows progress in using standard and nonstandard measures for length and area of objects.	Participates in creating and using real and pictorial graphs.
Explores/questions—Engages in open-ended explorations; forms questions that guide actions.						
Begins to investigate—Engages in simple investigations to extend observations, test predictions, and pursue questions.				✔	✔	✔
Collects data—Uses senses, varied tools, and simple measures to gather data.	✔	✔		✔	✔	✔
Records and represents experience—Describes and records experiences and information through a variety of means, including two- and three-dimensional representation, charts, and movement.	✔	✔		✔	✔	✔
Synthesizes and analyzes data from experiences—Sees patterns in data and relationships among experiences; makes reasonable predictions, explanations, and generalizations based on experience.	✔	✔	✔	✔		✔
Uses language to communicate findings—Develops increased vocabulary and ability to communicate observations and ideas.	✔	✔				
Collaborates—Shares materials, tasks, and ideas; collaborates in joint investigations.						

SOCIAL *and* SCIENCE	Demonstrates increasing capacity to follow rules and routines; uses materials purposefully, safely, and respectfully.	Increases abilities to compromise in interactions, take turns, and sustain interactions with peers by helping, sharing, and discussing.	Progresses in understanding similarities and respecting differences among people (such as gender, race, special needs, culture, and so on).	Develops growing awareness of jobs and what is required to perform them.
Explores/questions—Engages in open-ended explorations; forms questions that guide actions.	✓	✓	✓	✓
Begins to investigate—Engages in simple investigations to extend observations, test predictions, and pursue questions.	✓	✓	✓	✓
Collects data—Uses senses, varied tools, and simple measures to gather data.	✓	✓	✓	✓
Records and represents experience—Describes and records experiences and information through a variety of means, including two- and three-dimensional representation, charts, and movement.	✓	✓	✓	✓
Synthesizes and analyzes data from experiences—Sees patterns in data and relationships among experiences; makes reasonable predictions, explanations, and generalizations based on experience.	✓	✓	✓	✓
Uses language to communicate findings—Develops increased vocabulary and ability to communicate observations and ideas.	✓	✓	✓	✓
Collaborates—Shares materials, tasks, and ideas; collaborates in joint investigations.	✓	✓	✓	✓

Connections between Inquiry Skills and Outcomes in Other Domains (cont'd)

APPROACHES TO LEARNING and SCIENCE	Chooses to participate in an increasing variety of tasks and activities, developing the ability to make independent choices.	Approaches tasks and activities with increased flexibility, imagination, and inventiveness.	Grows in eagerness to learn about and discuss a growing range of topics, ideas, and tasks.	Grows in abilities to set goals and persist in and complete a variety of tasks, activities, and projects, despite distractions or interruptions.	Develops increasing ability to find more than one solution to a question, task, or problem.	Grows in recognizing and solving problems through active exploration, interactions, and discussions with peers and adults.
Explores/questions—Engages in open-ended explorations; forms questions that guide actions.	✓	✓	✓	✓		✓
Begins to investigate—Engages in simple investigations to extend observations, test predictions, and pursue questions.	✓	✓	✓	✓	✓	✓
Collects data—Uses senses, varied tools, and simple measures to gather data.		✓	✓		✓	✓
Records and represents experience—Describes and records experiences and information through a variety of means, including two- and three-dimensional representation, charts, and movement.	✓	✓	✓	✓	✓	
Synthesizes and analyzes data from experiences—Sees patterns in data and relationships among experiences; makes reasonable predictions, explanations, and generalizations based on experience.			✓	✓	✓	✓
Uses language to communicate findings—Develops increased vocabulary and ability to communicate observations and ideas.			✓	✓		✓
Collaborates—Shares materials, tasks, and ideas; collaborates in joint investigations.		✓			✓	✓

index

Other Resources from Redleaf Press

DISCOVERING NATURE WITH YOUNG CHILDREN
by Ingrid Chalufour and Karen Worth
Education Development Center, Inc.

The first unit in the innovative Young Scientist series, *Discovering Nature with Young Children* guides teachers through an inquiry-based curriculum that builds on children's natural curiosity about the living world around them.

DISCOVERING NATURE WITH YOUNG CHILDREN TRAINER'S SET
by Ingrid Chalufour and Karen Worth
Education Development Center, Inc.

This comprehensive trainer's set gives teachers an in-depth look—and visual tour—of the complete curriculum with discussion plans, sample charts and forms, resource suggestions, and a full-color video containing eight real-life vignettes of the curriculum in use.

HOLLYHOCKS AND HONEYBEES: GARDEN PROJECTS FOR YOUNG CHILDREN
by Sara Starbuck, Marla Olthof, and Karen Midden

This practical guide introduces teachers—with or without green thumbs—to the rich learning opportunities found in gardening with children.

MORE THAN MAGNETS: EXPLORING THE WONDERS OF SCIENCE IN PRESCHOOL AND KINDERGARTEN
by Sally Moomaw and Brenda Hieronymus

More Than Magnets takes the uncertainty out of teaching science. More than 100 activities engage children in interactive science opportunities—including life science, physics, and chemistry activities.

THE ART OF AWARENESS: HOW OBSERVATION CAN TRANSFORM YOUR TEACHING
by Deb Curtis and Margie Carter

Do more than watch children—*be*—with children. Covering different aspects of children's lives and how to observe them, as well as giving tips for gathering and preparing documentation, *The Art of Awareness* is an inspiring look at how to see the children in your care—and how to see what they see.

TRAINING TEACHERS: A HARVEST OF THEORY AND PRACTICE
by Margie Carter and Deb Curtis

Help teachers experience constructing their own knowledge and respecting their own learning styles so they can help children do the same. Some of the best ideas in teaching and learning are put into action with these innovative training tools.

OPEN THE DOOR, LET'S EXPLORE MORE!
FIELD TRIPS OF DISCOVERY FOR YOUNG CHILDREN
by Rhoda Redleaf

A complete guide for before, during, and after field trips that will help reinforce learning and make the most of your class adventures.

800-423-8309
www.redleafpress.org